GHOSTS

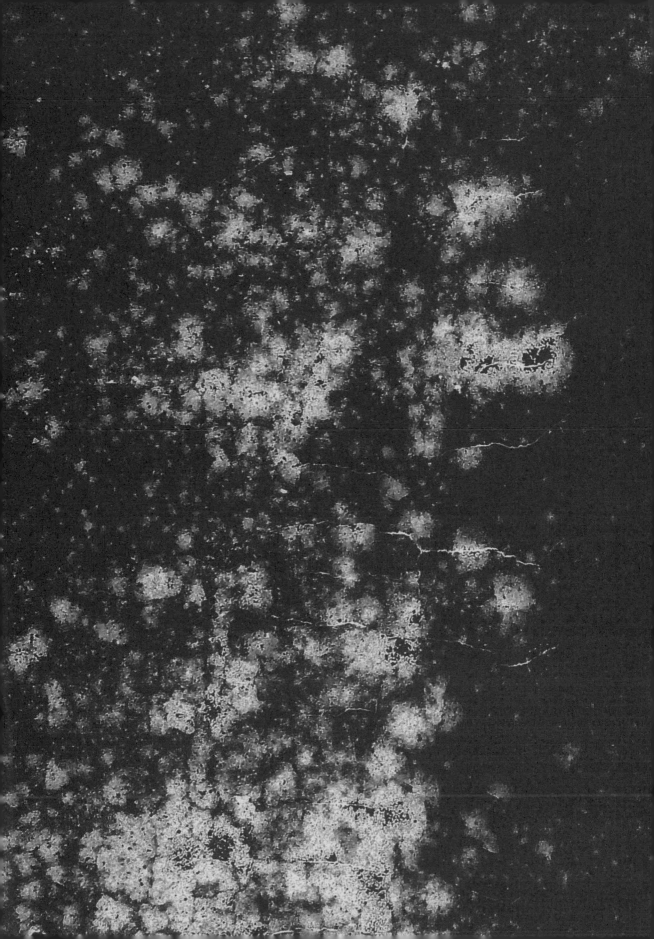

GHOSTS

TRUE CASES OF HAUNTINGS AND VISITATIONS

PAUL ROLAND

SIRIUS

SIRIUS

This edition published in 2024 by Sirius Publishing, a division of
Arcturus Publishing Limited,
26/27 Bickels Yard, 151–153 Bermondsey Street,
London SE1 3HA

ISBN: 978-1-3988-3729-4
AD011016UK

Printed in China

CONTENTS

INTRODUCTION

The belief in an immortal human soul or spirit and its survival after the death of the physical body is as old as humankind. It is shared by almost every culture and yet, there is still a substantial proportion of the population who doubt or deny the considerable empirical and anecdotal evidence supporting its existence.

This book provides compelling evidence of the existence of ghosts, while making an important distinction between the various manifestations of this fascinating phenomenon. The stories collected between these covers encompass such diverse natural phenomena as out-of-body and near-death experiences, crisis apparitions, phantom forerunners, bi-location and thought forms, as well as related supernatural phenomena, including poltergeists, spirit photography, possessed possessions and of course haunted houses, hotels and even entire ghost towns.

A few examples have been drawn from my own extensive personal experience and the rest from a lifetime study of occult phenomena. This has led me to an understanding that there is nothing to fear from investigating the supernatural and exploring the paranormal, provided that we can distinguish between a genuinely objective experience and one coloured/distorted by our personal expectations, beliefs and fears.

Why would one person see a ghost in its entirety and another see only a portion of it in the same location and at the very same time? Why do some apparitions interact with the living while others seem oblivious to our presence? If ghosts are conscious disembodied souls, how is it possible for us to glimpse an entire scene from the past? And if ghosts are mere echoes in the ether, why do some manifest to warn of danger, channel their talents through the living, or come back to convey a message from the world beyond?

Humankind has a fundamental need to believe in the immortality of the soul because it validates our own existence and gives us the hope and faith to endure the trials of life and the pain of loss. But if true ghost stories were merely chilling fairy tales and myths, they would not have endured through millennia and form the core belief of 57 disparate cultures, philosophies and religions.

It is true that orthodox Christianity does not profess belief in the immortality of the individual human spirit, nor the transmigration of the soul which is common to those traditions which espouse reincarnation, but esoteric Christianity does advocate the idea. As does that branch of esoteric Judaism known as Kabbalah which teaches initiates how to rise through the various stages of spiritual awareness 'in the spirit' using the central glyph of the Tree of Life.

Further back, in prehistory before the establishment of organized religion, our ancestors honoured their dead in expectation of an afterlife and attempted to communicate with their spirits and also the spirits of animal 'guides' through shamans, tribal elders, medicine men and high priests. Their practices for freeing the spirit survive in the rites and rituals of modern day shamans and pagans for whom the invisible world of disembodied souls and animism is as real, if not more so, than our physical world, for the other, they believe, is eternal while ours is transient.

The ancient Egyptians were obsessively preoccupied with the afterlife to such an extent that their religion was focused on making a cult of the dead, but in secret the high priests practised what today we would call astral projection to initiate neophytes in the mysteries of life and death.

Their custom of placing a mummified corpse into a series of sarcophagi of increasing refinement symbolized their belief that there are three non-physical components within the human body – the ka, ba and akh – which equate with the astral body of the Western esoteric tradition, the mind and the immortal soul. The astral body (also known as the etheric or dream body) is the matrix of energy which is effectively a blueprint for the physical form we assume on entering this material dimension at birth. And it is this incorporeal projection of our physical body that we call a ghost or apparition.

Beyond our physical bodies there may
exist an immaterial soul – from this
astral body come ghosts, apparitions
and other occult phenomena.

CHAPTER I

BELIEF IN THE SOUL

The belief in an immortal human soul and its survival after death dates back to prehistoric times and is common to almost every culture around the world.

In order to understand the nature of ghosts we need to accept the fact that we all possess what is often called a dream body – an etheric or spirit double composed of subatomic matter connected to our physical form by an etheric umbilical cord which is only severed upon death. Such a concept is central to the philosophies of the East, but can seem too fanciful to those Westerners who have not had an out-of-body experience (OBE), or at least have no memory of the experience, for it is likely that everyone has had an OBE during the deepest stages of sleep.

Evidence of a belief in immortality can be found in ancient burial customs which reveal that our ancestors had an expectation of an afterlife and a respect for the memory of the dead. This reverence for the departed, which dates back to the Stone Age and possibly beyond, is the clearest evidence that primitive man possessed self-awareness long before he had formed the means of expressing it in words. Prehistoric cave paintings from Africa to Australia support the belief that early man had a strong intuitive link with the spirit world and attempted to communicate both with his ancestors and with animals through tribal elders, shamans, medicine men and, later, the high priests of the first civilizations. Despite, by present standards, the inherent cruelty and comparative lack of sophistication of these early societies, it is evident that they all shared a belief in spirits long before the concept of good and evil found expression in orthodox religion.

Stonehenge – people have thought about the afterlife since the Stone Age.

Ancient rock art from Kakadu National Park, Australia. Early cave paintings reveal the existence of a strong connection between prehistoric man and the spirit world.

CULTS OF THE DEAD

The ancient Egyptians were so preoccupied with the prospect of an afterlife that their entire civilization was founded on the cult of the dead. Their custom of placing mummified corpses into sarcophagi of increasing refinement resulted from their belief that there are three non-physical components within the human body, (the *ka, ba* and *akh*) which equate with the etheric, astral or dream body of the Western esoteric tradition, the mind and the immortal soul. The etheric body is the non-physical counterpart that is effectively a blueprint for the form which our body takes on entering this material dimension.

Many believe that the pyramids may have been built not only as tombs for their pharaohs, who were venerated as living descendants of the gods, but also as the means of initiation into the mysteries of life and death. According to this interpretation, their alignment with specific constellations was chosen to provide a path through the sky for the ascending spirit of the pharaoh to journey back to the heavens, specifically the Sirius constellation in the Milky Way whose river-like pattern of stars appeared to be a celestial reflection of the Nile.

The imposing pyramids of Giza. It is possible that these were built to provide a path for the spirits of pharaohs back to the heavens.

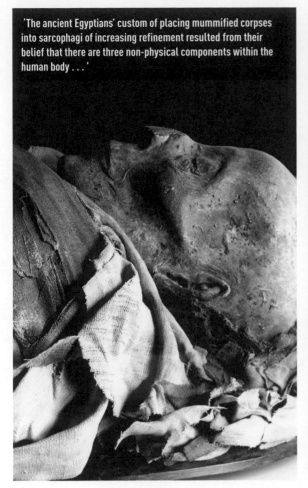

'The ancient Egyptians' custom of placing mummified corpses into sarcophagi of increasing refinement resulted from their belief that there are three non-physical components within the human body . . .'

One of the most famous works of art depicting doppelgängers – Dante Gabriel Roseetti's *How They Met Themselves* (1864).

It is also feasible that the empty stone sarcophagus in the King's Chamber of the Great Pyramid at Giza was used to stimulate the conscious separation of the soul in order for the high priests to be able to commune with the gods. The structural shape of the pyramids was believed to have both a mystical significance and a practical purpose, focusing the Earth's magnetic energies to a specific point and to such effect that the initiate would be unable to resist the force drawing their etheric body out of its physical home. Earth energies are stronger near water which suggests one explanation of why the pyramids were built near the Nile.

The Egyptian belief in the three spirit elements is significant because it has its equivalent in many cultures around the world which are different in virtually every other respect. It cannot be coincidence that the Greeks wrote of the significance of the *psyche*, the *pneuma* and the *nous*; the Muslims spoke of the *sirr*, *ruh* and

nafs; the Hindus acknowledged the *atman*, *jiva* and *pranamayakosha*; while the Jewish mystics contemplated the nature of the *neshamah*, the *ruah* and the *nefash* which the Christians assimilated and externalized in the concept of the Holy Trinity.

Belief in a spirit double which can free itself from the body during sleep and exist separate from the body also gave rise to the Roman *larva*, the German *doppelgänger*, the English *fetch*, the Norwegian *vardoger* and the Scottish *taslach*.

Today belief in a spirit double is shared by cultures as diverse as the Azande in Africa, the Inuit of Alaska and the Bacairis in South America as well as the major religions and philosophies of the East. Clearly there must be a basis in fact for this shared belief. It seems unlikely that mere wishful thinking or the desire to deny our own mortality could account for the consistency of such beliefs.

SACRED SPIRITS

In many parts of the world, ghosts are not considered to be a creation of local folklore, but a fact of life. In China the dead are understood to co-exist with the living, a belief which gave rise to the practice of ancestor worship, while in South America the deceased are honoured with annual festivals known as the Day of the Dead which suggests that the material world and the spirit world might not be as distinct as we like to believe. In many Eastern religions, it is believed that death is not the end, but simply a transition from one state of being to another. The Hindu Upanishads, for example, liken each human soul to a lump of salt taken from the ocean which must ultimately return to the source.

In Buddhism, the personality is believed to dissolve at the moment of death, leaving only pure consciousness (rupa) to seek a new body unless the individual was an enlightened soul (bodhisattva) in which case it can ascend to the higher states of being and there choose when to intervene in the lives of the living as a guiding spirit. However, those individuals who are as yet unable to free themselves from earthly attachments may descend into the realm of the hungry ghosts, the Buddhist equivalent of the Christian hell. It is implied that the majority of discarnate souls linger in a limbo between lives, known as the bardo, before reincarnating.

More than 1,000 years ago, monks in East Asia described three phases of death which are uncannily similar to modern accounts of the near-death experience. The first stage, called chikai bardo, occurs when consciousness is suspended at the point of separation from the physical body. At this moment the individual is unaware that they are dead. Only when they look down on their own lifeless body do they realize that this ethereal essence is their true self.

They also stressed the importance of letting go of all emotional attachments to people and places so that the soul may ascend into the light. But some may be unwilling, or unable, to relinquish their possessions or may harbour regrets or resentment which will

The witch of Endor, whom Saul consulted with to summon a spirit.

by the Old Testament (Deuteronomy 18:9–14), but conscious awareness of the higher worlds for the purpose of self-realization or enlightenment had been practised since biblical times by initiates of Merkabah, a forerunner of the modern Jewish mystical teaching known as Kabbalah.

Spirits are not acknowledged explicitly in the New Testament although their existence is clearly implied, most notably in Luke 24:39, when Jesus tells his followers: 'Touch me and make sure that I am not a ghost, because ghosts don't have bodies, as you see that I do!'

Elsewhere, particularly in the 'lost' Gnostic gospels discovered at Nag Hammadi in 1947, there are several significant references to the living spirit within every human being and to the disciples' personal experience of the astral world and altered states of awareness. In the Gospel of Philip, Jesus makes a clear distinction between 'the real realm' (i.e., the material world) and 'the realm of truth'. In 1 Corinthians 15:50

and 2 Peter 1:18 it is stated that flesh and blood cannot enter the celestial kingdom; in John 3:13 it is noted that heaven is for spiritual beings and that we are all spirit in essence and will return from whence we came.

According to the Gnostic gospels, Jesus appeared to his followers as a spirit to prove that the soul survives death, but due either to selective editing of the gospels or a mistranslation of the rich metaphorical language of the Gnostic gospels, this central teaching became literalized. St Paul attempted to clarify the idea that Jesus had risen physically from the tomb and in so doing made a distinction between our earthly form and our spirit.

Elsewhere, in 2 Corinthians, St Paul speaks of having attained separation of the spirit and the body at will and having ascended 'in the spirit' to the third heaven, which was a technique he may have mastered as an initiate of an aesthetic sect of Jewish mystics who practised Merkabah – an advanced form of meditation which translates as 'rising in the chariot'.

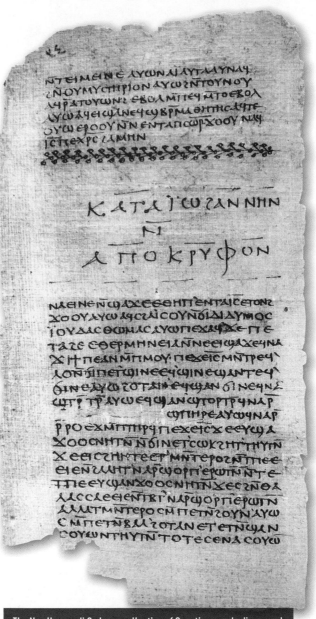

The Nag Hammadi Codex, a collection of Gnostic gospels discovered in 1947, refers to experiences of the astral world.

RESTLESS SPIRITS

In South America there is the legend of the Weeping Woman who is said to have committed suicide after a handsome seducer refused to marry her as he had promised to do. She is said to haunt the highways in search of her children whom she had killed in order to be free to marry him. Her tale is told to young girls entering womanhood as a warning against believing the lies of men. In Japan there is a long tradition of apocryphal ghost stories in which wronged women return from the dead to take their revenge on those who have dishonoured them. The tale of the Tofu Seller is characteristic of this type of fable. It tells of a blind tofu vendor who is tricked into removing a charm from the door of a house by a wizened old hag who claims to be the ghost of the householder's first wife. Once the charm is removed, the ghost glides inside and a horrible scream is heard from within as the old hag frightens her husband's second wife to death.

The most persistent ghost story in Japanese culture is the legend of the *Kuchisake-onna*, the spiteful spirit of a vain young girl who was the wife or concubine of a jealous samurai in the Heian period. Fearing that she had betrayed him with another man, he is said to have disfigured her and then taunted her by saying: 'Who will think you're beautiful now?' Her face covered with a mask, the *Kuchisake-onna* wanders through the fog seeking solitary children, young men and women, whom she asks: '*Watashi kirei?*' (Am I beautiful?). If they answer 'yes' she tears off the mask and asks again. If they keep their nerve and again answer 'yes' she allows them to go on their way, but if they run screaming she pursues them, brandishing a long-bladed knife or a scythe. If she catches a man she butchers him and if she catches a girl she mutilates her, turning her into another *Kuchisake-onna*. The story is so deeply rooted in the Japanese psyche that as recently as 1979 there was public panic when it was rumoured that the *Kuchisake-onna* had been seen attacking children. In 2004, cities in South Korea were rife with similar rumours.

The earliest credible account of a spectral encounter was recorded by the Greek philosopher Athenodorus who lived during the 1st century BC. Against the advice of his friends, Athenodorus agreed to rent a room in a lodging house that was reputed to be haunted because it was cheap and he wished to prove that his actions were determined by his intellect and not his emotions. At nightfall his nerves were tested by the appearance of a gaunt-faced spirit of an old man draped in the soiled vestments of the grave. The spectre was weighed down by chains and appeared to be in anguish but was unable to communicate what it was that bound him to that place.

The philosopher kept his nerve and indicated that he was willing to follow the ghost wherever he wished to lead him. It led Athenodorus along a narrow passage and out into the garden whereupon it faded into the bushes. Athenodorus noted where the spirit had disappeared and the next morning he informed the magistrates, who ordered workmen to excavate the garden. There they unearthed a skeleton weighed down by rusted chains which they assumed was that of a murder victim. They then had the skeleton reburied according to Greek funeral rites. Such stories have their counterpart in virtually every culture from ancient times to the present day.

The English ghost story tradition can be traced back to an episode involving Lord Lyttleton who, in 1779, claimed that he was tormented by the spirit of his jilted mistress, Mrs Amphlett, whose three daughters he had also seduced. She had committed suicide in despair and had returned to foretell the day and hour of his death. His friends, fearing for his sanity, thought they would try to outwit the spook by turning all the clocks forward. When the appointed hour passed without incident his lordship retired to bed much relieved and cursing himself for being a superstitious fool. But the dead are not so easily cheated and at the appointed hour Lord Lyttleton expired in his sleep from a fit.

'"Watashi kirei?" (Am I beautiful?)' The legend of the Kuchisake-onna resurfaced in South Korea in 2004.

La Llorona, the weeping woman of South American tradition.

WHAT IS A GHOST?

Ghosts are not a supernatural phenomenon but a purely natural one. It is generally accepted that they are either earthbound spirits or residual personal energy which lingers at a location which was significant to the individual in life or at the moment of their death. Our fear comes from our vain attempts to deny the existence of these apparitions and not from any power that they can hold over the living.

Colorado-based parapsychologist Jeff Danelek

THE UNAWARE GHOST

Some entities may remain within the physical realm simply because they are not aware that they are dead and go on about their life much as they did before until some sudden trauma causes them to realize that they have died.

THE DENIAL GHOST

There are personalities who will refuse to accept the truth of their own earthly demise. They can be the ones who remain earthbound the longest, for human pride can be as powerful and debilitating on the other side as it often proves to be on this side of eternity, which can make it especially difficult to convince them to give up the charade and move on.

THE ATTACHED GHOST

This type of ghost is so emotionally attached to the things of the world that it refuses to let go of them. This is often their home or some place they truly loved. And so they stay behind, always hovering on the edge of human perception, but rarely if ever able to interact with it in any meaningful way. Such ghosts often remain around for years, or even decades.

has become something of a ghost-hunters' guru after presenting a compelling argument for the existence of spirits in his influential study, *The Case For Ghosts* (Llewellyn, 2006). In place of the usual sensationalistic stories of playful poltergeists and other paranormal phenomena, Jeff approaches the subject in an objective, down-to-earth manner that has earned him the respect of both the scientific community and other paranormal investigators. He has identified various categories of ghost which he believes equate with recognizable personality types.

THE JEALOUS GHOST

Though exceedingly rare, there are accounts of ghostly entities attaching themselves not to things, but to people, and interjecting themselves into earthly relationships, usually out of some misguided notion of possessiveness or outright jealousy. This could be anything from an over-possessive spouse that can't accept the thought of their mate remarrying, to a spurned lover who took his or her own life only to come back and attach themselves to the source of their unrequited affections later. Active only around the source of their possessiveness, the jealous ghost can be among the most tenacious and frightening ghosts of all.

THE FEARFUL GHOST

Some personalities are simply too afraid to find out what fate has in store for them and so prefer the mundane existence of a haunting to the potential punishment of a final judgement. Often these are individuals who did considerable harm – or believe they did – to others and so fear being held to account. It's not just evil-doers who find themselves in this state, however, but ordinary people who have had strong religious beliefs drilled into them and feel they have not lived up to them.

THE MELANCHOLY OR SAD GHOST

The 'sad' ghost is someone who is so overwhelmed by some tragedy that they continue to wander the physical realm as if in a state of shock that they seem unable to recover from. Suicides often end up as 'sad' ghosts. The same factors that drove them to take their own lives frequently keep them bound to the physical realm. They are the most lost of all souls and may require significant intervention on both the part of the living and other spiritual entities to pull them towards the light.

THE MISSION GHOST

This type of ghost stays around in order to take care of some unfinished business that was cut short by their unexpected death. This 'mission' can be as simple as revealing the location of a hidden will, or as major as trying to find justice for a life cut short by murder, but in either case mission ghosts seem intent upon achieving some goal they've set before themselves and feel they cannot rest until they have succeeded.

THE GOODBYE OR COMFORT GHOST

The goodbye ghost is a manifestation that appears – often only once – to either say goodbye to a loved one bereaved by their loss or to simply assure them that they are well and have passed over successfully. These can manifest as electrical phenomena or something as dramatic as a full-body manifestation. Tales of widows seeing their late husbands sitting on the foot of their bed or children encountering the manifestation of their dead sibling in their bedroom are legion.

THE CURIOUS GHOST

Those who are of a scientific bent might find the chance to manipulate matter and energy from the other side to be too good an opportunity to pass up. Such personalities, however, are fairly rare and frequently frustrated in their efforts to get through to us 'thick mortals', so may move on to explore other realms of the spirit.

THE ANGRY GHOST

Angry personalities may be willing to endure the personal hell of an earthly wandering in search of vengeance. Such entities are relatively rare, but even so they present the greatest challenge to the ghost-hunter. Anger is a destructive force that grows more powerful with time and can only be dissipated through the power of love and compassion.

THE MISCHIEVOUS GHOST

Similar to the curious ghost but of a more menacing vein is the mischievous or 'playful' ghost. It is interested in simply frightening the living and finds haunting to be one great amusement. Such ghosts are immature and childish (like the personalities behind them) and are comparable to the practical joker. Their actions can range from moving furniture to hiding jewellery to pulling the sheets off a bed or even physical assault! They may be the source of at least some poltergeist activity.

ANGELS AND APPARITIONS

The vengeful ghost has become a cliché of graphic horror fiction and films. But in reality it seems that a restless spirit can do little more than appear looking melancholic and hope that it will prick the conscience of the guilty party into making a full confession, or persuade a kindly soul to restore its reputation. Ghosts have also been known to warn of danger and even to take control of endangered ships and aircraft, guiding their pilots and passengers to safety.

ACCUSED FROM BEYOND THE GRAVE

In January 1897 Mary Jane Heaster of Greenbrier, West Virginia was grieving for her daughter Zona who had died in mysterious circumstances earlier that month at the age of 23.

The official cause of death was recorded as being 'complications resulting from childbirth', but Mary Jane was adamant that her daughter had not been pregnant. Zona had, in fact, given birth to an illegitimate child two years earlier, but it was preposterous to suggest that her health had been compromised to such an extent that she could have succumbed as a result.

Mary Jane was not satisfied. Her suspicions had been further aroused by the testimony of the attending physician, Dr Knapp, who was also, coincidentally, the coroner. He had been summoned to Zona's home on the fateful night to find that her husband of just three months, Edward (Erasmus) Shue, had moved the body to an upstairs bedroom and had re-dressed her in her finest Sunday clothes.

He was in a severely agitated state, cradling his new bride's lifeless body in his arms and wailing as melodramatically as a music hall villain. He refused to allow the doctor to examine her closely, insisting that he be left in peace to grieve. He claimed to know nothing of the circumstances that had led to her death as the body had been discovered by a young boy whom he had sent to the house on an errand. It was the boy who had found her lying lifeless downstairs and had run for help.

All Edward would say was that she had succumbed to an 'everlasting fit'. Under the circumstances Dr Knapp could do nothing more than catch a cursory glimpse of the dead woman's face, which he observed had a marked discoloration on the right cheek and on

On four successive nights Zona's earthbound spirit manifested in her mother's house.

the neck consistent with a blow and strangulation.

At the wake Edward's erratic behaviour aroused further suspicion. He refused to allow any of the mourners to approach the casket and had covered the marks on her neck with a scarf which he claimed had been her favourite.

It was quite by chance that her mother happened to remove a white sheet from the coffin just before the burial. Perhaps it was female intuition or a whisper

from beyond the grave. Whatever compelled her to recover the sheet it was to prove a defining moment in the case.

THE INDELIBLE STAIN

The first thing Mary Jane noticed was the odd odour which she had initially attributed to embalming fluid, but the more familiar she became with that smell, the more convinced she became that it was something else, something indefinable. When she tried to rinse the sheet the water turned the colour of blood. Scooping some of it out with a jug, she was astonished to see it was as clear as drinking water, yet the water in the bowl remained crimson red. The sheet was no longer white, but pink, the colour of diluted blood.

No matter how hard she scrubbed the sheet and no matter how long she soaked it, the stubborn stain remained. The only thing Mary Jane could do now was pray. She demanded answers, for if denied she knew she would lose her mind from grief. In the following days when the dying light of day had receded and the shadows lengthened her prayers were answered.

On four successive nights Zona's earthbound spirit manifested in her mother's house and revealed how she had suffered at the hands of her abusive husband. On the night of 22 January he had flown into a rage when he learned that she hadn't cooked meat for his dinner. He beat her and broke her neck. And to prove it, the apparition turned its head around 360 degrees! Had anyone inspected the body they would have seen the incriminating bruising and felt the dislocated vertebra in the neck. But as no post-mortem had been performed there was no evidence to support the mother's suspicions, other than the accusation of a ghost.

EXHUMATION

Nevertheless, Mary Jane marched over to the office of the local prosecutor, John Alfred Preston, and demanded that he put the question to her former son-in-law. Preston couldn't order Edward's arrest on hearsay evidence at the best of times and certainly not on that allegedly provided by a ghost. But he had his doubts concerning Edward's version of events and was only too willing to have Zona's body exhumed for an autopsy. Edward's evident distress at the news seemed to confirm what everyone in the town had been saying for weeks – that he had taken her life and, therefore, he couldn't be permitted to get away with it.

The autopsy confirmed that the real cause of death was strangulation, which was all the prosecutor needed to instigate proceedings. Edward was immediately arrested and while he paced up and down his tiny cell in the county jail further investigations unearthed his chequered past. Proof was obtained of two earlier marriages, one of which ended in divorce and the other with the 'accidental' death of the second wife who had been killed by a blow to the head. Apparently three wives

were not enough for Edward, who boasted to his fellow inmates that he intended to chalk up seven marriage partners before he settled down to an ignominious old age. He was confident that no jury would convict him. After all, what evidence could they have? No one had actually seen him murder his wife. An intruder could have done it. All he needed to do was sow sufficient reasonable doubt and he'd walk out of the courtroom a free man.

He had heard rumours of Zona's ghost, but dismissed it out of hand as the ravings of a grief-stricken mother. Unfortunately for the prosecution, testimony pertaining to the ghost was ruled inadmissible by the judge even before the trial got under way. When Edward walked into the courtroom on the first day of the trial it was all he could do to suppress a smug grin.

THE TRIAL

Edward's attorney shared his client's over-confidence and that was his undoing. He thought he would have some fun at Mary Jane's expense by asking her to repeat her ghost story in the belief that it would discredit her in the eyes of the jury. But she remained calm throughout the questioning, impressing both the jury and the judge. Nothing the defence could say seemed to sway her. It was not her imagination, she assured the court, that had told her that her daughter had been killed by having her breath choked out of her and her neck 'squeezed off at the first vertebra'. That was the first time that the precise cause of death had been mentioned during the proceedings and when it was subsequently confirmed by the physician who had written the autopsy report there was a hushed silence in the courtroom. Edward was caught in a web of deceit and subsequently convicted of murder. The only reason he escaped execution was the fact that he had been convicted on circumstantial evidence and not the word of an eyewitness. He died in prison on 13 March 1900 and is the only man to have been convicted of murder in the United States on the testimony of a ghost.

Elva Zona Heaster Shue, murdered in 1897, returned to haunt her killer and even found a way to give testimony at the trial through her mother.

GHOST SHIPS

Such incidents are often attributed to echoes in the ether, but there have been many cases where ghosts have actively intervened to save the living. In 1949 the captain of the passenger liner *Port Pirie* was on shore in Sydney, Australia awaiting orders while the crew were giving the ship a last look over in preparation for their next voyage.

One of the engineers filled the boiler and turned the pumps off when the gauge indicated that the boiler was full. But as he walked away the pumps started up by themselves. After double-checking the gauge he turned the pumps off again and turned away, but again the pumps turned themselves back on. Now that his curiosity had been aroused he stripped down the boiler and gave it a thorough overhaul. He discovered that the gauge was faulty and had been registering that the boiler was full when it was almost empty.

Had the ship been allowed to sail with this fault undetected it could have resulted in a fatal explosion at sea with the loss of all hands. When the engineer told his crewmates about this one of them remembered that it had happened before. The ship's first chief engineer had been killed after the boiler had run dry and blown up.

The ghost ship *Pamir* – grateful survivors swear it exerted a 'mysterious force' which pulled them into calmer seas.

THE DOOMED U-BOAT

On a darker note, the crew of German submarine *UB-65* appear to have been doomed from the moment their U-boat was built. During its first voyage a torpedo exploded while being loaded aboard, killing six men and the second officer. But this was not the last time the officer was seen aboard. While it was on its first patrol the crew reported seeing the officer standing on deck with his arms folded and looking up into the clouds. He was seen again the day the captain was killed and thereafter whenever some disaster struck the vessel. The mere appearance of the phantom was sufficient to drive one sailor into committing suicide by jumping into the sea although nothing untoward had actually occurred that day. On its final fateful voyage in 1918 it was sighted apparently abandoned on the surface by a US submarine, *L-2*, whose captain ordered his crew to action stations in the belief that it was a trap. But before he could fire on it the U-boat exploded and sank beneath the waves. The last thing the American captain noted in his log was the appearance of a German officer standing motionless on the hull, his arms folded and looking upwards into the sky.

GHOST FLIGHT

Executives of American carrier Eastern Airlines were literally haunted by their past when they decided to reuse parts salvaged from a crashed Tristar Lockheed L-1011 to repair other planes in their fleet. Their troubles began in December 1972 when Flight 401 fell out of the sky over the Florida Everglades claiming more than 100 lives including the pilot, Bob Loft, and flight engineer, Don Repo.

Within months of the crash, members of the cabin crew were reporting sightings of both men on their flights and these were augmented by sightings from passengers who had been disturbed by faint but full-length figures, subsequently identified as Loft and Repo from their photographs. One female passenger became hysterical when she saw the man in the seat next to her disappear. He had looked so pale and listless that she had called an attendant to see if he was ill. The attendant arrived just in time to see the man disappear before her eyes. He had been dressed in an Eastern Airlines uniform and was later identified from photographs as Don Repo.

On several occasions the pair have taken an active interest in the flight. A flight engineer was halfway through a pre-flight check when Repo appeared and assured him that the inspection had already been carried out. One particularly persuasive account was recorded by a vice president of Eastern Airlines who had been enjoying a conversation with the captain of his Miami-bound flight from JFK until he recognized the man as Bob Loft. Needless to say, the apparitions played havoc with the schedules. When the captain and two flight attendants saw Loft fade before their eyes they hastily cancelled the flight.

Usually the pair appear simply to check that all is well but on one particular flight they intervened to prevent a potentially fatal accident. Flight attendant Faye Merryweather swore she saw Repo looking inside an infrared oven in the galley and called the flight engineer and the co-pilot for assistance. The engineer immediately recognized Repo's face, then they heard him say, 'Watch out for fire on this airplane.' The warning proved timely. During the flight the plane developed serious engine trouble and was forced to land short of its destination. The oven was subsequently replaced to appease the cabin crew, who were becoming increasingly unsettled by such incidents.

This and other episodes are a matter of record in the files of the Flight Safety Foundation and the Federal Aviation Agency. The former investigated several incidents and concluded: 'The reports were given

The Tristar Lockheed L-1011 that crashed in December 1972.

by experienced and trustworthy pilots and crew. We consider them significant. The appearance of the dead flight engineer [Repo] . . . was confirmed by the flight engineer.'

The airline responded to the intensifying interest in their planes by refusing to co-operate with anyone other than the airline authorities. It appears they have learnt the true meaning of 'false economy'. The story inspired a bestselling book, *The Ghost of Flight 401*, by John G. Fuller and a 1978 TV movie of the same name starring Ernest Borgnine and the then unknown Kim Basinger.

GUARDIAN ANGEL IN DISGUISE

By no means all ghosts are out for revenge or to right an injustice. Some appear to be guardian angels in disguise. One of the most remarkable cases was that reported by British pilot Bill Corfield, who flew into a terrible thunderstorm en route to Athens in 1947. As the plane and its crew were buffeted by high winds and visibility was severely reduced, Bill had little choice but to take them down to 20 metres above sea level and fly blind in the hope of breaking through the clouds.

Just then his navigator spotted the Corinth Canal, an extremely narrow passage only 5 metres (16 ft) wider than the wing of the plane. Instinctively Bill banked into the mouth of the canal and levelled off, flying in the pitch dark for 7 km (4.3 miles), a manoeuvre Bill later admitted was 'suicidal'.

But no one panicked. In fact, the crew were overwhelmed by a sense of serenity that one compared to being in a cathedral. Bill admitted, 'I knew – absolutely and without doubt – that my brother [Jimmy who had been killed in World War II] was with me in the aircraft. There was nothing physical [to see] but he was there.'

So convinced was he of his brother's presence that Bill took his hands off the steering controls and let his brother pilot the plane. It was only when they were clear

SPINNING IN HIS GRAVE

In the autumn of 1916 a flight training school in Montrose, Scotland was the scene of a series of hauntings which seem to support the belief that a spirit will return from the world beyond if it feels compelled to right a wrong or seek recognition it believes it deserves.

For several months a vaguely discernible figure attired in a pilot's uniform was seen outside the mess hall by senior members of staff. It would approach the door of the hut then vanish. Inside meanwhile, pilots and staff would describe having sensed a presence. One even swore that he saw the spectre standing at the foot of his bed. Subsequent research concluded that the ghost must have been that of flight instructor Desmond Arthur, who had been killed during a routine flight in 1913 as the result of a botched repair to his biplane. The error had apparently been covered up and the accident attributed to pilot error which must have had Arthur spinning in his grave for as soon as the true facts came to light, the haunting ceased and Arthur presumably returned to his rightful resting place.

of the canal and in clear skies that Bill took back control and delivered the plane and its grateful crew to their destination.

THE LAST FLIGHT

Ghost ships have long been a staple ingredient of salty sea tales and ghost trains are said to have been sighted on more than one abandoned railway line, but phantom planes are a distinct rarity.

Early on the morning of 13 June 1993 air traffic controllers at John Wayne airport, in Orange County south of Los Angeles, were besieged by calls from pilots complaining that a private plane was invading their airspace, posing a serious risk to both inbound and outgoing aircraft.

Its shrill engine sent three noise monitors into the red and annoyed the ground staff who noted its FAA (Federal Aviation Administration) number so they could lodge a formal complaint. People living in the exclusive properties surrounding the airport had also been driven to distraction. They'd been phoning the authorities all morning to voice their anger that a maverick pilot was being allowed to disrupt their breakfast, buzzing

their homes and performing aerobatics too near to a residential area.

In fact, he had been flying so low that several irate citizens had noted the FAA number painted on the distinctive red fuselage, N21X. Within the hour, the registered owner had been identified. It was Donald 'Deke' Slayton, a former Mercury astronaut, captain of

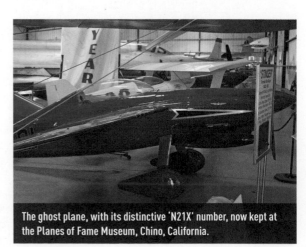

The ghost plane, with its distinctive 'N21X' number, now kept at the Planes of Fame Museum, Chino, California.

the 1975 Apollo-Soyuz mission who was known to have an insatiable appetite for speed.

But he was nobody's hero that morning. As his plane finally climbed into the clouds and faded from the radar screens, muttered curses and annoyance was all that trailed in his wake. It was not only a damn nuisance, it was a highly irresponsible stunt and more than a few residents were determined to pursue their complaint through the FAA until they got a result. It wasn't long in coming.

Two weeks later a letter of censure against 'Deke' Slayton was approved and three weeks after that it was finally delivered to his wife Bobbie. Only she wasn't his wife any longer. When she called the FAA to ask them what kind of sick joke they thought they were playing, she made it very clear indeed that she was Deke's widow and she was angry with good reason. She had been with him that morning at his bedside hundreds of miles away in Texas as he lay dying from brain cancer.

And no, no one else could have borrowed the plane as it was on display in an aeronautics museum in Nevada on the day in question, stripped of its engine.

NASA astronaut Donald 'Deke' Slayton, who couldn't possibly have flown the plane on 13 June 1993.

CHAPTER 2

THE NIGHT SIDE OF OF NATURE

The modern preoccupation with the paranormal could be said to have begun in 1848 with the publication of *The Night Side of Nature*. The Victorians were avid readers of ghost stories, but they bought this collection in unprecedented quantities because its author, Scottish novelist Catherine Crowe, appealed both to their romanticism and their reason. Her obvious delight in describing Gothic horrors was balanced with rigorous research. Each episode was backed up by witness statements, documents and dates to reinforce the author's belief that the supernatural was as worthy of serious investigation as the natural sciences. By insisting that at least two independent witnesses corroborate each sighting, she laid down the ground rules for conducting paranormal research which was to change little over the next 100 years.

WILLINGTON MILL

Her most thorough and intriguing investigation concerned a haunted mill house owned by an industrialist, Joshua Proctor, near Newcastle upon Tyne, England, called Willington Mill. The property was only 40 years old when Proctor moved in during the spring of 1840, so it did not conform to the traditional idea of a house haunted by the spirits of previous owners. Moreover, Proctor was a devout Quaker, a God-fearing Christian not given to belief in spooks. And neither was Dr Edward Drury, a hardened sceptic and amateur ghostbuster who was the first on the scene when rumours of the haunting circulated around the region. In July, Drury and his trusted friend Mr Hudson inquired if they could spend the night in the mill house in order to 'unravel the mystery'. Proctor clearly believed that something was amiss and had even sent his family away so that the investigators could have a clear field.

At 11 pm on the night of 3 July 1840, Dr Drury and his companion made themselves comfortable on a third-floor landing outside the haunted room and settled down for an all-night vigil. At midnight they heard the sound of bare feet running across the floor, then knocking sounds as if someone was rapping with their knuckles on the bare boards. Other noises followed in quick succession – a hollow cough and a rustling – suggesting that a presence was making itself known. At 12.45 am, Dr Drury saw a sight that was to haunt him for the rest of his life. A closet door swung open and 'the figure of a female, attired in greyish garments, with the head inclining downwards, and one hand pressed upon the chest as if in pain', strode slowly towards him. The spectre advanced towards Mr Hudson, at which point the doctor found the courage to charge at it but he passed right through the apparition, knocking over his companion. Drury confesses that he recollected nothing for three hours afterwards and was assured by Hudson and Proctor that he was 'carried down stairs in an agony of fear and terror'. The good doctor was so traumatized by his experience that he required ten days to calm his nerves before writing his account. He ended it by stating that he had gone there as a devout disbeliever but had emerged convinced of the reality of the supernatural.

Not content with relying on Dr Drury's account and Proctor's verification, Mrs Crowe dug deeper, unearthing accounts of earlier and subsequent sightings at Willington Mill given by four other people, plus a local newspaper proprietor and a historian who discovered that ghosts had been seen in a house that had occupied the same site 200 years earlier. Mrs Crowe wrote:

The appearance presented was that of a bare-headed man in a flowing robe like a surplice, who glided backward and forward about three feet from the floor, or level with the bottom of the second-storey window seeming to enter the wall on each side and thus present a side view in passing. It then stood still in the window and a part of the body came through both the blind which was closed down and the window, as its luminous body intercepted the framework of the window. It was semi-transparent and as bright as a star, diffusing a radiance all around. As it grew more dim it assumed a blue tinge and gradually faded away from the head downward. Had any magic lantern been used it could not possibly have escaped detection . . .

Willington Mill, the site of a Victorian ghostly mystery.

THE FOX SISTERS

The event that led to the birth of the spiritualist movement occurred in Hydesville, near Rochester, New York in the spring of 1848. On 31 March, a Methodist farmer named James Fox, his wife Margaret and their two daughters, Margaretta aged 14 and Kate aged 12, retired early in the hope of catching up on their sleep. They had suffered several disturbed nights due to noises which they assumed were caused by the wind rattling the shutters of their wooden-framed house. But the wind was not to blame. Before coming to bed Mrs Fox tried the sashes to see if they were loose and was answered by bangs for which there was no obvious explanation. Puzzled, she put the children to bed then prepared to retire herself. The family all slept in the same room and so Mrs Fox was a witness to what happened next. The rapping noises began again. Kate reminded them all that the next day was April Fool's Day and assumed that someone was playing a practical joke. She thought it might be fun to test them and challenged whoever was making the noises to copy her. She snapped her fingers and was immediately answered by the same number of raps. Then Margaret clapped and was answered in the same way. By now Mrs Fox was concerned as she knew that no one else but her husband could be in the house and he would not indulge in such frivolous games. She was also aware that a previous tenant had moved out after complaining of inexplicable noises. She later wrote:

I then thought I could put a test that no one in the place could answer. I asked the noise to rap my different children's ages, successively. Instantly, each one of my children's ages was given correctly, pausing between them sufficiently long to individualize them until the seventh (child), at which a longer pause was made, and then three more emphatic little raps were given corresponding to the age of the little one that died . . .

The Fox sisters (l to r) Margaretta, Kate and Leah.

Mrs Fox kept her composure, but she was increasingly anxious. She asked out loud if it was a human being making the noises. There was no reply. 'Is it a spirit?' she asked. 'If it is make two raps.' She was answered emphatically with two bangs that shook the house. In later weeks, disbelievers accused the children of making the noises by cracking their joints but it is reported that anyone who had heard the loud reports which shook the walls that first night would have dismissed such explanations out of hand.

Emboldened by her ability to converse with the other side, she then asked if it was an 'injured spirit' to which she received two loud raps in reply. Using an impromptu code, Mrs Fox elicited the following information from the intruder. It was the spirit of a 31-year-old man who had been murdered in the house and had left behind a widow and five children. Mrs Fox obtained permission from the spirit to invite the neighbours in to witness their exchange, but many were too frightened to enter the bedroom. They waited outside while a hard-headed pragmatist by the name of William Duesler sat on the end of the bed and quizzed the spirit with more personal questions. Duesler's cynicism melted the moment the bed vibrated in response to the strength of the rapping sounds.

Duesler managed to draw out more information including the fact that the murdered man was a peddler by the name of Charles Rosma and that he had been killed five years earlier by a previous tenant of the house, a Mr Bell, for the $500 that he had saved and carried with him. Subsequent inquiries confirmed that a maid had been sent away on the evening a peddler had been invited to spend the night, and that when she returned the next morning the peddler had gone.

By Sunday, 2 April, rumours of what was taking place in the Fox family home were the topic of conversation around every breakfast and dinner table in the town. Hundreds of people converged on the house hoping to hear the raps and learn the latest news from the spirit world. Interest intensified when it was learnt that the murdered man had informed the family that his body had been buried in their cellar. Without

The wooden house at Hydesville where the Fox family lived was photographed and visited by hordes of visitors fascinated by the tales of communication with the spirits of the dead.

delay James Fox and a number of men collected picks and shovels and started digging up the dirt floor. The excavation had to be interrupted when they struck an underground stream, but a couple of months later the water had drained away and digging was resumed. Five feet down they struck a plank. Underneath they discovered human bone fragments and tufts of hair in a bed of quicklime.

Meanwhile, the previous owner, Mr Bell, had been traced to nearby Lyon, New York, but in anticipation of being accused of murder he had petitioned his neighbours to provide written testimony as to his good character. There was little that the law could do at this stage other than wait for more damning evidence to be unearthed – or for Mr Bell to be forced into making a confession by his conscience or by the persistent phantom. Curiously, the murdered man had predicted that his killer would never be brought to trial and it proved to be so.

But then, in November 1904, the cellar wall collapsed, revealing the original wall behind it and between the two, a skeleton. Someone had evidently exhumed the body from its initial grave beneath the cellar floor and re-interred it behind a hastily built partition. It was all

A skeleton had been buried in the cellar of the Fox family home and hidden by a hastily built partition.

reminiscent of a scene from Edgar Allan Poe. But who was the victim? Those who looked upon it were in no doubt, for next to the grisly find lay a peddler's tin box.

THE BIRTH OF SPIRITUALISM

The Fox family were the first people to become national celebrities in the field of spiritualism. Not surprisingly, there were those who resented the attention they had attracted, specifically the Church authorities who were suspicious of anyone claiming direct communication with the dead. Under pressure from the Church, three separate committees were set up in the following months to investigate the phenomena. They subjected the children to strip searches and tests in which they tied their ankles together and made them stand on pillows to isolate them from the floor, but still the rappings continued. All three committees concluded that the children attracted the anomalous activity even if they were not the cause of it. When the children were absent from the house, nothing happened. The children

were separated and sent away to stay with relatives. Yet still the noises continued.

A 16-year-old girl, Harriet Bebee, who visited the boarding house, was disturbed to discover that the spirits followed her home to plague her and her family. The Fox family were finally forced to abandon their besieged home and move to Rochester, where the eldest of the three sisters, Leah, lived, but to their dismay the spirits pursued them to their new house where the rappings persisted. Some were so loud that they could be heard at the other end of town.

Such an epidemic of poltergeist ('noisy ghost') activity suggests that at least some of the phenomena might have been produced by the children themselves – teenage girls have subsequently been found to be the origin of much psychokinetic activity (physical phenomena caused by involuntary discharges of psychic energy) due to physiological changes at puberty – rather than by the sudden incursion of angry spirits into one region of the country.

Smoke and mirrors or the real thing? The Fox sisters began charging people to come to watch the antics of their visiting spirits and were soon earning a very good living.

However, some of the mischievous antics can only be explained in terms of spirits. One such spirit identified himself through decoded communications with Kate as a dead relative by the name of Jacob Smith. The deceased were evidently keen to communicate, but were limited to creating loud reports and throwing objects across a room. Attempts were made to create a more sophisticated alphabetical code using different knocks to identify specific letters but any form of communication which relied on a crude form of Morse code was laborious and unreliable. A new and more direct way had to be found. The answer lay in allowing the spirits to take over the body of a willing individual so that the spirit could speak through their voice boxes or guide their hand to write a message from the world beyond.

The age of the medium was at hand.

An illustration showing the early stages of the Fox sisters' activities. One of the girls speaks to the spirit in the Hydesville home, while the rest of the family look on.

A SURPLUS OF SPIRITS

Mediums were nothing new. Since prehistoric times shamans, witch doctors, holy men and priests had claimed to be able to commune with their ancestors and the gods. In some cases it is clear from the nature of their messages that they were expressing ideas from their own subconscious and that the gods from whom they channelled their laws and edicts could be seen to have been universal archetypes personifying aspects of their own psyche. Many, however, appeared to be genuine channels for discarnate entities whose predictions and insights were later verified by subsequent events.

But psychic sensitivity and its various manifestations – clairvoyance ('clear seeing'), clairaudience ('clear hearing') and clairsentience ('sensing an unseen presence') – are not the exclusive preserve of 'gifted' mystics. Everyone, to a greater or lesser degree, has the ability to attune to the presence of spirits.

In the wake of the Fox sisters' experience, hundreds of ordinary people across the United States and Europe began holding séances and many were shocked to discover that they too could produce loud reports and automatic writing, and move objects. More than 100 'mediums' appeared in Rochester alone in a single year. Newspaper reporters across the country were run off their feet chasing

Séances were the natural off-shoot of the rise of spiritualism, and were often taken part in by way of a diverting after-dinner parlour game.

stories of spectral manifestations and levitating tables.

Two brothers and a sister named Davenport who lived in Buffalo, New York, had been disturbed by loud reports and vibrations in 1846, but they did not understand their significance until they attended a séance held by the Fox family four years later. During one of their own séances, Ira Davenport was told by a spirit to fire a pistol. In the flare of the discharge, witnesses swore they saw the ghostly figure of a man with his finger wrapped around the trigger. After the shot, the pistol was snatched out of Ira's hand and it fell to the floor. The spectre, who identified himself as 'John King', subsequently entered the bodies of each of the brothers and spoke through them for all in the room to hear.

Soon spirits across the country were performing all manner of 'tricks' for the amusement of spellbound onlookers: playing musical instruments, moving furniture, producing ectoplasm (a gelatinous substance drawn from the living essence of matter), manifesting objects in mid-air (apports) and even superimposing their faces on that of the medium – a phenomenon known as transfiguration. It was as if the disembodied had suddenly discovered a way to tear the veil between their world and this and were as excited and uninhibited as children who had just learned to ride a bike.

Spiritualism swiftly became a recognized religion. In spiritualist meetings a medium would deliver a sermon dictated from the spirit world and then pass on messages from the departed to the eager congregation. However, the mysteries of life and death and the nature of the world beyond were rarely alluded to in anything other than the vaguest of terms. The spirits seemed preoccupied with mundane matters and 'unfinished business' on Earth. It was as if they were trapped in a limbo between the worlds, unable to move on so long as their loved ones refused to let them go. For the bereaved it was undoubtedly comforting to be given indisputable evidence of survival in the form of personal information that no one else but the

A publicity illustration for the Davenport Brothers and their cabinet: the scale of the apparent activity has been exaggerated – in reality the men were out of sight during most of the show.

deceased could have known, but for those seeking answers to life's mysteries it was ultimately unsatisfying. Perhaps spiritualism wasn't the breakthrough it had promised to be.

The Church was outraged and condemned all communication with the beyond as dabbling with the Devil. As their pews emptied, they took courage from the numerous accounts of fake mediums who had been exposed by the press and they vented their righteous indignation on those fraudsters who had preyed on the bereaved and the gullible. But despite the damage done to its reputation, the new movement continued to spread at a phenomenal rate. Even Queen Victoria and Prince Albert declared themselves convinced after enjoying a table-turning (the manipulation of a table during a séance, attributed to spirits) session at one of their country retreats. While some treated a séance as nothing more than a fashionable new party game to amuse their dinner guests, and the scientific establishment dismissed the whole business on principle, there was also a sense that something significant had come to light. Perhaps science and religion no longer had all the answers.

THE HAUNTING OF CHARLES DICKENS

The Victorians were very fond of ghost stories and the most popular authors of the period relished competing with one another to see who could make their readers' flesh creep the most. One of the era's best-loved storytellers was Charles Dickens. In fact, he was a hardened sceptic until he had a disquieting paranormal experience of his own.

In 1861, Dickens contributed a ghost story to the popular magazine *All The Year Round* which centred on an encounter between a portrait painter and a young lady in a railway carriage. During the journey, the story goes, the lady asked whether the artist could paint a portrait from memory. Two years later, an elderly gentleman by the name of Wylde commissioned the artist to paint a portrait of his daughtwer from a description as she was not available to sit for the portrait in person for she had died some time earlier. After several failed attempts to capture her likeness, he recalled the young woman whom he had met on the train and used her as his inspiration. 'Instantly, a bright look of recognition and pleasure lighted up the father's face,' Dickens wrote, 'and he exclaimed, "That is she!"' When the artist asked when the young lady had died, he was told it was on the very date the painter had met the pale young woman on the train.

Such twists were almost clichés even in Victorian fiction, but what makes this particular story significant

In Dickens' story, an artist encounters a phantom and is later commissioned to paint her portrait.

is that it was to have a resonance in real life. Shortly after publication, Dickens received an irate letter from a painter who claimed that the story was not fiction, but fact. It had been his own personal experience which he had written down with the intention of submitting it for publication, but had delayed and he was now convinced that Dickens had heard his story somehow and copied it – even down to the date chosen for the girl's death. The painter had told the story to his friends but had never mentioned the date until the time he wrote it all down. This is what particularly unnerved Dickens. He later wrote, 'Now my [original] story had no date; but seeing when I looked over the proofs the great importance of having a date, I wrote in, unconsciously, the exact date on the margin of the proof!'

Charles Dickens was accused of plagiarism for his ghost story from 1861 by a painter who claimed to have told the exact same story to his friends.

GHOST LIGHTS

Not all spirits appear in human form. Often entities will register on video film and photographs as moving lights. Reverend Charles Jupp, warden of a Scottish orphanage, recorded the following story in 1878:

I suddenly awoke without any apparent reason, and felt an impulse to turn round, my face being turned towards the wall, from the children. Before turning, I looked up and saw a soft light in the room. The gas was burning low in the hall, and the dormitory door being open, I thought it was probable that the light came from the source. It was soon evident, however, that such was not the case. I turned round, and then a wonderful vision met my gaze. Over the second bed from mine, and on the same side of the room, there was floating a small cloud of light, forming a halo like the brightness of the moon on an ordinary moonlit night. I sat upright in bed looking at this strange appearance, took up my watch and

found the hands pointing at five minutes to one. Everything was quiet, and all the children sleeping soundly. In the bed, over which the light seemed to float, slept the youngest of the . . . children mentioned above.

I asked myself, 'Am I dreaming?' No! I was wide awake. I was seized with a strong impulse to rise and touch the substance, or whatever it might be (for it was about five feet high), and was getting up when something seemed to hold me back. I am certain I heard nothing, yet I felt and perfectly understood the words – 'No, lie down, it won't hurt you.' I *at once* did what I *felt* I was told to do. I fell asleep shortly afterwards and rose at half-past five, that being my usual time.

PHANTOMS IN PHOTOS

In the second half of the 19th century, the North American city of Boston was buzzing with talk of technological advances that promised to transform it into a modern metropolis to rival New York and Washington, DC. The First Transcontinental Railroad would soon link the Eastern Seaboard with California to unite a nation that was still in mourning after five years of civil war. Meanwhile, inventions such as electricity and the telegraph promised a life of faster communication and greater comfort and convenience. Into this heady whirl of progress and expectation emerged the new science of photography.

Boston photographer William Mumler did not set out to prey on the bereaved by promising to capture the spirit of their loved ones on film, but he saw how eagerly they queued at his studio to have their portraits taken. Few complained that he charged five times more than his competitors, but then no one else offered their clients the possibility of a 'reunion' with their deceased loved ones that could be photographed for posterity.

In 1861, while developing a plate in his darkroom, Mumler, a former jewellery engraver, had chanced on what appeared to be a new phenomenon, 'spirit photography'. The photo he was working on was a self-portrait, but it had a blemish of some kind which, when printed and examined in daylight, was revealed to be the likeness of a young girl. Mumler showed it to a friend as a curiosity and joked that the mysterious figure was that of his dead cousin. To his astonishment, his friend assumed he was serious and urged him to send the photo to a leading spiritualist publication, the *Banner of Light*, which duly published it as irrefutable evidence that spirits could be seen by the new science. Photography was still a relative mystery to the general public, who assumed that the camera recorded only what it saw. Photographic phenomena, effects and tricks of the light were then unknown. Few people considered that the picture might be a fake or an accidental double exposure.

A BOOMING BUSINESS

Whatever misgivings Mumler might have entertained were cast aside when he saw the busy waiting room at his Washington Street studio in the days following the picture's publication. His wife Hannah, a clairvoyant, didn't need much persuading to aid him in the deception. She engaged the clients in small talk while they waited their turn and then passed on the information to her husband, so that he could make his performance behind the camera more convincing. He was the 'channel' for the spirits and his wife was the medium who drew them from the world beyond. But there was no guarantee at all that the dead would comply. Often clients would leave with only a conventional family portrait and the hope that the deceased would put in an appearance at a subsequent sitting – for another $10.

Mumler's rivals were not so naïve, however, and were incensed that he was turning their profession into a freak show. They had their suspicions about how he achieved his phantom effects, but proving them was another matter. The whole affair was complicated by the fact that fake phantom photography had become a fashionable business, with stereoscopic cards of 'ghosts'

Photography was an exciting new technology that gripped the imagination of later-19th-century America. It was not long before the market was flooded with purported photographs of ghosts and other spirits.

The front page of the spiritualist newsletter, the *Banner of Light*.

and 'devils' being offered for the amusement of the middle classes, who purchased them as a novelty item.

In 1863, Mumler invited Dr Child, a Philadelphia physician, to study his methods and put an end to the growing rumours that the phenomenon was nothing more than an effect achieved by double exposure, trick lenses, reflections or concealed accomplices dressed as 'apparitions'. The latter was a favourite trick of fraudsters, who capitalized on the fact that their sitters were required to remain absolutely still while the shutter remained open for up to a minute. This gave ample time for assistants to appear and disappear, leaving a ghostly impression on the plate.

CLOSER INSPECTION

Dr Child visited the Boston studio with several friends who oversaw the entire process, from the preparation of the plates to the developing of the prints. They also examined the equipment and made a thorough search of the studio for compartments where an accomplice could be hidden. To eliminate the chance that the plates might be switched at some stage, Dr Child marked each of them with a diamond but still Mumler produced his phantom portraits, to the astonishment of the sceptics.

Yet the doubters would not be persuaded. That same year the physician, poet and essayist Oliver Wendell Holmes Snr. wrote a damning exposé of spirit photography in the influential magazine *The Atlantic Monthly*. He poured scorn on those who were duped into accepting such images as genuine as well as those who fabricated them for profit.

As a result of the article, Mumler's clients took a closer look at their precious 'evidence'. Several of them realized that there was something suspiciously familiar in the faint impressions, which bore a striking similarity to photographs of their loved ones taken while they were alive. Prominent spiritualists who had previously greeted the photographs with enthusiasm also began to question their authenticity, and were forced to examine their faith in the movement when told that several of the 'spirits' were very much alive and well and living in Boston!

Mumler quietly left town and he set up business on Broadway in 1868. Evidently, news of his chicanery hadn't filtered through to New York, where he enjoyed a roaring trade, encouraged by a flair for shameless self-publicity. Mumler was prone to exaggeration, but it is estimated that he must have taken around 500 photographs by this time, which, at $10 a sitting, amounted to a considerable sum. But his satisfaction was short-lived – in March 1869 several members of the Photographic Section of the American Institute of the City of New York took their suspicions to the press and demanded an investigation into his activities.

One of Mumler's photographs, showing a 'ghost' lurking behind the man sitting for the photograph.

BROUGHT TO COURT

A few weeks later, Joseph Tooker, an undercover police officer posing as a grieving client, paid for a portrait with a deceased relative. When Mumler failed to produce the goods, Tooker arrested him and threw him into the notorious city prison known as the 'Tombs'.

Incredibly, when Mumler emerged to stand trial on 21 April, he found the courtroom packed with spiritualists offering moral support to the man they felt had produced irrefutable evidence validating their beliefs. It was clear from the hostile and mocking tone adopted by the press that it was not only Mumler on trial, but the spiritualist movement itself. *The New York Times* poured scorn on the women who packed the public gallery and filled the court 'with a cold and clammy atmosphere… worn down [by] ethereal essences'. Other publications declared Mumler 'a stupendous fraud'.

But if the prosecution thought they had ample evidence to convict, they were mistaken. Tooker's testimony was soon overwhelmed by a series of defence witnesses who swore on oath that Mumler had provided them with proof of life after death. One of the most convincing was Charles Livermore, who identified the spectral image in a photograph as that of his late wife. He declared that several of his friends were also prepared to testify to the fact. He had even tried to put Mumler to the test by arriving a day early for his sitting to foil any preparations the photographer might have been making to produce the desired effect. During the sitting he altered his pose in order to 'defeat any arrangement he might have made… I was on the lookout all the while'. Perhaps the most dramatic testimony was given by a former justice of the New York Supreme Court, Judge John Edmonds, who confessed that he communed with the dead during murder trials. He claimed that they provided him with details of how they had died and whether the accused had done the foul deed. Judge Edmonds was in no doubt that Mumler's photographs were genuine.

A HOLLOW VICTORY

Sensing defeat, the prosecution called several photographic experts to the stand to explain how the effects might have been produced. One of them observed that the Livermore 'ghost' cast a shadow, which no ethereal phantom should do. Furthermore, the shadow was cast in the opposite direction to that of the living subject, indicating that there were two separate light sources and that two separate pictures had been taken at different times of the day. The conflicting shadows could not possibly have been cast at the same time.

To conclude, the prosecution called the celebrated carnival showman P.T. Barnum, who boasted that he knew a conman when he saw one. The accused had allegedly sold Barnum a collection of spirit photographs which the showman had put on display in his museum of curiosities. The merchandise had come with an incriminating letter in which Mumler had admitted faking the photographs – or so Barnum claimed, for he had lost the letter in a fire.

On 3 May Mumler took the stand and asserted, 'I have never used any trick or device, or availed myself

Boston in the 19th century.

of any deception or fraud.' Following this, the defence summed up by implying that the case was nothing less than a witch hunt – Mumler was being persecuted for his 'faith'. Judge Dowling was not persuaded and declared he was convinced that Mumler had defrauded his clients – but as the prosecution had not proven how the deception had been achieved, he had no choice but to set the photographer free.

It was a hollow victory, however, for Mumler was now deep in debt and unable to pay his legal bills. He returned to Boston to live as a lodger with his mother-in-law and there carried on his work, defiantly claiming that he alone could capture the spirits of the deceased on camera. He died in 1884, reviled by the photographic profession which accused him of bringing the new science into disrepute, and after having destroyed his entire archive of negatives, presumably in an effort to remove the evidence of his deception.

The showman P.T. Barnum was not so easily taken in by Mumler's claims.

PHOTOGRAPH OF A PRESIDENT

If Mumler was a fraud, he was also a significant figure in the history of photography. He is now credited with several innovations (which he patented), including Mumler's Process, which enabled photographs to be reproduced in publications with no loss of detail. In spite of his sullied reputation as a spirit photographer, his photographs are still of historical interest. His most famous photograph, taken in his cramped Boston studio in 1871, shows an elderly woman dressed in mourning. But the photo also shows her 'husband' standing behind her, his hands resting on her shoulders. The lady's name is Mary Todd Lincoln and the apparition is the late president, Abraham Lincoln. Mary had unmasked several fake mediums, but she had recently been to a séance where her dead husband had communed with her and she wanted to have her photograph taken in the hope that he might appear again. A staunch believer in spiritualism, she accepted the 'evidence' of the photograph without question, but to the trained eye it is clearly a fake.

Mumler's photograph of Mary Todd Lincoln, with its visage of the dead president standing behind her.

THE FACE IS LIKE THAT OF A DEAD PERSON

Across the Atlantic, an English photographer was attracting attention by claiming to produce similar phenomena. Unlike Mumler, Frederick Hudson had the backing of a respected medium, Mrs Guppy, whose ringing endorsement guaranteed him a steady stream of clients who would not look too closely at his pictures. But others were not so willing to suspend disbelief, among them professional photographer John Beattie, who persuaded Hudson to participate in a controlled experiment and to consent to the results being published in the *British Journal of Photography*.

Hudson's garden studio was a large, converted greenhouse, which also served as his darkroom. After the camera equipment and plates were examined, Hudson seated himself with his profile to the camera while his daughter stood next to him, acting as medium. The first photograph showed nothing unusual, but for the second portrait the girl retreated to the background and

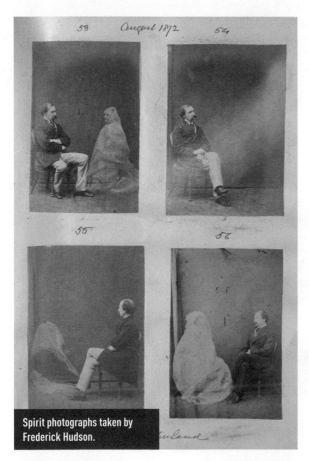

Spirit photographs taken by Frederick Hudson.

this time a third seated figure appeared on the print. A third photograph produced another apparition, 'a standing female figure, clothed in a black skirt, and having a white-coloured, thin linen drapery something like a shawl pattern, upon her shoulders, over which a mass of black hair loosely hung.'

Beattie still had his doubts about the authenticity of the images, but he couldn't figure out how Hudson had achieved the results. However, there was one explanation he hadn't considered, perhaps because it was just too simple. Hudson had switched the plates. Such a trick must have aroused suspicion among critics within the spiritualist movement, because in September 1872 they began voicing their doubts in the pages of the *Spiritualist* magazine, accusing Hudson of double-printing two separate plates or preparing his plates in advance. They cited a photograph in which the pattern of a carpet could be seen superimposed over the fabric of a sitter's clothing, an anomaly that could only have occurred if the carpet had been on the first exposure with the fake spirit.

By this time, the pages of the 'yellow press' were full of sensational exposés of fraudulent mediums and their theatrical parlour tricks. The favourite manifestation was ectoplasm, a dense misty miasma said to indicate the presence of a ghostly spirit. To achieve this effect, a roll of cheesecloth would be teased out of the medium's mouth or dropped down from the ceiling on a string at the climax of the séance.

GENUINE PHOTOGRAPHS

In the 1890s, just as spirit photography looked as though it had lost all credibility, support came from a most unexpected source. J. Traill Taylor, editor of the *British Journal of Photography*, published a series of articles in which he and his staff revealed how certain ghostly effects could be achieved, but they also suggested that some photographs may have been genuine after all. Using a stereoscopic camera to prove his theory, Taylor discovered that 'genuine' images remained two-dimensional and, he argued, they would not have done so had they been faked double exposures.

The following year, Alfred Wallace, co-creator of the theory of evolution, also came to the defence of spiritualism and spirit photography, arguing along the same lines as Taylor. Just because many photographs were obvious fakes, he wrote, it did not mean that they all were, and consequently photos of dubious veracity should be examined scientifically.

ONE LAST LOOK ROUND

One example of a 'genuine' spirit photo deserving of serious study is commonly known as the 'Lord Combermere Photograph'. Taken in 1891 by amateur photographer Sybell Corbett in the library of Combermere Abbey, Cheshire, it appears to show the faint, glowing figure of a man seated in what Sybell swore had been an empty chair. The exposure was made during the course of an hour and Sybell, who was staying in the house at the time, went to great lengths to ensure no one entered the room while the picture was being taken. The servants would not have dared to sit in the chair, even if they had managed to sneak in. Besides, there was no question as to the chair's occupant; the family and servants identified the figure as Lord Combermere himself. The only problem was that his Lordship was being interred in the family vault at the same time as the picture was being taken. But perhaps the fact that the photograph was taken on the day of his funeral only adds to the validity of the image. What better time for a ghost to take one last look round his ancestral home?

The Lord Combermere Photograph, showing the ghostly figure of a man sitting on a chair at the left of the image.

PHOTOGRAPHING THE INVISIBLE

In the first decade of the new century, many other inexplicable photographs were published in the mainstream press as well as in spiritualist periodicals – so many, in fact, that books began to appear on the subject. The first bestseller was *Photographing the Invisible* (1911) by James Coates, which made a compelling case for the camera as the new medium for preserving fleeting appearances of the recently deceased. The book was such a success that it was republished ten years later in a considerably expanded edition and is thought to have prompted a series of rigorously scientific experiments devised and monitored by American photographer Charles Cook.

In 1916, Cook put two 'spirit photographers', Edward Wyllie and Alex Martin, to the test, providing them with his own plates and insisting that the negatives be developed by a commercial studio to prevent deception. Cook was convinced that the images the two men produced were genuine and that their rare psychic faculties had helped to conduct the spirits' etheric energy on to the photographic plates. For this reason, he preferred to call the results 'psychic photography', a term that suggested the phenomenon was attributable to the mediumistic abilities of the photographer rather than the camera. His theory was supported by Columbia University's Professor James Hyslop, who endorsed the publication of Cook's study with an enthusiastic introduction that attracted interest from within the academic establishment.

Among the most notable studies was the one undertaken by the eminent British chemist Sir William Crookes of the Royal Society, himself a keen amateur photographer. Sir William spent several years examining all the evidence he could accrue and came to the conclusion that much of what he had seen supported the case for psychic phenomena and spirit photography. However, the more frequently he affirmed his beliefs, the greater the scorn he suffered from colleagues, who accused him of being a credulous eccentric who had lost sight of his scientific principles.

A spirit photograph by Edward Wyllie.

Renowned British chemist, Sir William Crookes, who believed the evidence supported the existence of the paranormal.

A couple poses along with a mysterious figure in one of William Hope's photographs. Hope eventually admitted that he doctored his photographs.

A CONFESSION

Matters were not helped by the activities of the Crewe Circle in the 1920s. William Hope, their de facto leader, made great show of offering prospective clients the opportunity to provide their own photographic plates; however, no one seemed suspicious when he demanded that they leave them in his studio overnight so that they could be 'magnetized' to make them more sensitive to etheric presences!

Hope was frequently accused of fraud and sleight of hand – primarily swapping plates during the handing out of hymn books – but he was never caught. However, he once admitted to Archbishop Thomas Colley, a fervent believer in the supernatural, that he had doctored his photographs. Hope claimed to be a medium and boasted that he could channel the spirit of the archbishop's late mother; but he mistakenly used the wrong image on the plate and confessed to the deception in an attempt to avoid prosecution. To his relief, the archbishop was more than charitable, declaring that the old woman in the photograph was indeed his mother. Colley even put a notice in the local paper, inviting those who remembered his mother to call at the rectory to identify her from a selection of photographs that included Hope's 'mistake'. Eighteen people duly confirmed that the unknown woman was the archbishop's mother, and the incident provided Hope with much-welcome publicity as well as an enthusiastic new patron.

After losing his son and brother in the Great War, the novelist Arthur Conan Doyle had become a convert to the spiritualist cause. He sprang to Hope's defence after the celebrated ghost-hunter, Harry Price, questioned the veracity of several of Hope's photographs. Price and Conan Doyle were friends, sharing a passion for the paranormal and maintaining an affectionate rivalry, but the heated dispute over Hope's claim to be a genuine medium blighted their relationship. Years later, it came to light that a member of Hope's circle had found a flash lamp and cut-out faces with which the 'medium' had produced his effects. Had this been known at the time, Doyle and Price may have remained friends and Hope would have been exposed.

A MAGICIAN AMONG THE SPIRITS

Another of Conan Doyle's fellow seekers was the celebrated escapologist and illusionist Harry Houdini. It is not generally known that Houdini began his career as a fake medium. However, he soon realized how dishonourable the practice was when he lost a close member of his family and yearned for genuine contact with the deceased. Ashamed of his own small part in the 'great deception', Houdini began a comprehensive investigation and in 1924 published his damning conclusions in a book called *A Magician Among the Spirits*. He had attended countless séances and considered none of them to be genuine; he went on to produce a rational explanation for every form of spectral manifestation he had witnessed, including table rapping, automatic writing and apports (the manifestation of physical objects). His enthusiastic debunking of the paranormal did not endear him to Conan Doyle and others who refused to have their unshakable faith questioned.

Compelling evidence against spirit photography was mounting and deception was becoming more difficult. The public were generally less gullible than they had been during the height of the spiritualist craze and the various tricks and crude effects that had been perpetrated upon them were now widely known and easier to identify.

THE BROWN LADY AND OTHERS

Almost a century later, the photographs that survived scrutiny remain tantalizing glimpses of a new frontier of paranormal research. One such example was the 'Brown Lady of Raynham Hall'. This apparition is remarkable not only because it has defied rational explanation since

Hope would swap out photographic plates to make his spirit photography possible.

Scourge of the phoney spiritualists: Harry Houdini poses for a fake spirit photograph in order to demonstrate how the forgeries were produced. Photos such as this were highly popular until the trickery involved was revealed to the public.

the picture was taken in September 1936 by *Country Life* photographer Captain Hubert Provand, but also because his assistant, Indre Shira, actually saw the ghost descending the staircase. Shira had urged Provand to take the picture, which duly depicted what the assistant described ('a vapour form which gradually assumed the shape of a woman in a veil'). Provand admitted that he hadn't noticed anything at the time, which suggests that Shira was the more psychically sensitive of the two (assuming, of course, that the photograph is not a fake). Both men were considered reliable witnesses, not given to practical jokes. The ghost is thought to be Lady Dorothy Walpole, who died in 1726 of a broken neck caused by being pushed down the staircase by her husband after he learned of her affair with another man. She is known as 'the Brown Lady' because her spirit has been seen on several occasions wearing a brown brocade dress.

Between the wars, many supposed 'spirit photographs' were subjected to examination by experts at the leading photographic equipment manufacturer Kodak, who presumably knew a fake when they saw one. Even they failed to find evidence of natural phenomena or fraud in some of the photographs they were asked to assess. There was also the testimony of witnesses who appeared to have nothing to gain from

deceiving the public and everything to lose if exposed. Three of the most famous phantom photographs of the post-war years were taken by men of the cloth. The first of these was a colour picture taken by the Reverend R.S. Blance in 1959 at Corroboree Rock in the Australian outback, 160 km (100 miles) from Alice Springs. The site was said to be the location of Native Australian rituals involving animal sacrifice. The photograph shows a translucent woman emerging from the bush. Reverend Blance was not aware of anyone else in the area at the time.

The second photograph, taken in the 1960s by the Reverend K.F. Lord, captures a hooded figure on the steps of the altar at Newby Church in Yorkshire, England. Reverend Lord stated that he didn't see anything at the time and was only photographing the empty sanctuary for his album.

The third image, commonly known as 'the Greenwich Ghost', was snapped in 1966 by a Canadian cleric, the Reverend R.W. Hardy at Queen's House, Greenwich, London. It shows a shrouded figure ascending the Tulip Staircase. All three photographs were scrutinized by experts who assumed them to be fakes, but who subsequently ruled out the possibility of a hoax, a reflection or flaws in the camera or on the film.

Raynham Hall, home to 'the Brown Lady', the ghost of Lady Dorothy Walpole.

Reverend Hardy's photo of the ghost on the Tulip Staircase of the Queen's House, Greenwich.

THE PHANTOM PASSENGER

A typical photograph that defied explanation was taken by Mrs Mabel Chinnery in 1959. Mrs Chinnery was visiting her mother's grave in an English churchyard when she decided to photograph it; she then took a separate photo of her husband who was waiting in the car. Although he was alone in the vehicle at the time, the print clearly shows the ghostly presence of an elderly woman in the back seat. The couple identified the mystery woman as Mabel's late mother and offered both the print and the negative to experts at a national newspaper, who declared themselves satisfied that neither had been tampered with.

However, one respected expert, Dr Eric John Dingwall (1890–1986), who devoted 60 years of his life to studying the paranormal as an author and chief researcher for the Society of Psychical Research (SPR), remained unconvinced. Dingwall was a firm believer in ghosts and other paranormal phenomena, but he had found fault or fakery in almost every spirit photograph he was asked to examine. When he could not discern any fault, he contended that there must be a rational explanation even if he couldn't provide one. Dingwall's suspicions cannot be easily dismissed, as he repeatedly cautioned against scepticism and was widely respected in psychic circles as a diligent observer and a man who prided himself on keeping accurate records.

In a private letter to parapsychologist Guy Playfair in 1976, Dingwall stated his views: 'We know practically nothing about the "real" nature of the material world in which we live… the more we peer into our surroundings the most indefinite becomes the boundary. The investigation of the relationship between matter and what you call spirit is only just beginning…. The scrapheap of science is high with discarded theories derived from insufficient experimentation.'

Mabel Chinnery's photo of her husband and the ghost of her mother sitting in the back seat.

REAL OR FAKE?

There are arguably more fake spirit photographs and phantom film clips now than at any time since the phenomenon came to light, because such images are so easy to create today. Almost every schoolchild knows how to use a computer to manipulate images and edit video. However, among the obvious hoaxes there are occasional images that defy rational explanation.

The much-published shot of the 'uninvited guest' at a holidaymaker's farewell party in 1988 is one such example. In this picture, a group of guests are seated round a table at the Hotel Vier Jahreszeiten in Maurach, Austria. To take the photo, a camera was set up on an adjacent table and the timer was primed, but when the shutter clicked the flash failed to trigger. A second shot was set up and this time the flash fired. When the prints came back from the laboratory the group discovered they had a new member – the head of a young woman can clearly be seen materializing at the edge of the table. Her head is noticeably larger than those of the other guests and she is slightly out of focus. This would suggest that her image comes from a previous undeveloped shot, making the photograph an accidental double exposure – yet neither the photographer nor anyone else at the party recognized the woman. The Royal Photographic Society and the photographic department at Leicester University subjected both the print and negative to rigorous tests and concluded that it was not a case of double exposure.

The 'Guildhall Monk' is another example. In January 1985, St Mary's Guildhall was the setting for a formal dinner hosted by the Coventry Freemen's Guild. As the guests bowed their heads in prayer, a photograph was taken. When it was developed, the group of guests had been joined by a tall, hooded figure in what looked like a monk's habit. The mayor affirmed that no one had attended the dinner dressed in that fashion, and none of the other guests recalled seeing a person in such clothes. It is worth noting that the building dates from the 14th century and served as a prison for Mary, Queen of Scots.

The ghost of a monk is said to haunt St Mary's Guildhall.

THE PHANTOM PILOT
AND THE WOMAN IN WHITE

The 'Phantom Pilot' is another case that appears to substantiate belief in ghosts. In 1987, Mrs Sayer and a group of friends were visiting the Fleet Air Arm Station at Yeovilton in south-west England. Mrs Sayer was persuaded to sit in the cockpit of a helicopter and have her picture taken. She remembers it was a hot summer's day, yet she felt cold sitting in the co-pilot's seat. Of the number of snaps taken, only one came out and it showed a hazy figure in a white shirt sitting in the pilot's seat next to Mrs Sayer. The helicopter had seen action in the Falklands War, but it is not known whether or not the pilot had been killed.

The 'Woman in White' is another convincing example. On 10 August 1991, Mari Huff, a member of the Ghost Research Society, took a photograph at Bachelor's Grove Cemetery near Chicago. The cemetery was noted for occurrences such as strange lights, unearthly sounds and sightings of hooded figures, so the GRS brought cameras loaded with high-speed infrared black-and-white film that was acutely sensitive to low light sources. The GRS saw nothing extraordinary until Mari's film was developed. Her photo clearly shows a young woman dressed in white, sitting on a tombstone. She appears to be brooding and her dress is old-fashioned and semi-transparent. It looks like a 'classic' ghost photo of the kind that might adorn a book jacket, but Mari and her colleagues swear that this is what the camera 'saw' that day.

With the advent of digital photography and image manipulation software, one might think that spirit photography is an anachronism from a more innocent age. But photographs purporting to show glowing orbs, blurred shadowy figures and milky-white phantoms continue to appear in periodicals and on the internet. The fact that some of these images have been subjected to analysis by sophisticated software and declared 'genuine' (or at least 'un-tampered with') only intensifies our enduring fascination with paranormal phenomena. We all know how such effects are created and how easily we can be deceived, but it seems we still need to believe in the paranormal because we live in hope of a better life – for many of us, the life that begins after our present one ends.

Bachelor's Grove Cemetery near Chicago, Illinois, has been the source of numerous paranormal occurrences.

SIMULACRA

A final word of caution, before you are tempted to see ghostly faces and figures in your own family photographs. The human brain is wired to identify patterns so that we can recognize familiar faces and distinguish friend from foe. The problem is that we often 'see' faces where there are none. An example of this is the famous 'Face on Mars', which prompted wild speculation among purveyors of the 'ancient astronaut' theory that there was now irrefutable evidence of the remains of pyramid-like structures on the planet's surface. It was later revealed to be nothing more than a play of shadows. This is such a common phenomenon that scientists have given it a name, matrixing (or pareidolia), and the illusory objects it produces are known as simulacra.

One of the most macabre examples of a simulacrum is that of the 'Tennessee Electric Chair'. When the state penitentiary decided that 'Old Sparky' needed modifying, the job was given to local engineer Fred Leuchter, who had it delivered to his basement workshop. The chair had been made of timber from the local gallows, so it had violently despatched more than its share of miscreants and no doubt some poor innocent souls too, making it a prime candidate for a haunting. Leuchter took several photographs before he began his work. In some of these there are luminous orbs, which could be reflections; but something that appears to be a human hand grips an armrest on the chair, although it has been suggested that this, too, is a reflection. One image in particular invites a second look – that of a face at the back of the chair. The strangest aspect is the size of the face, which is much smaller than a human head would be if a living person occupied the chair. Remember, in the Austrian party photograph described on page 62, the disembodied head of the 'uninvited guest' was notably larger than those of the other people seated round the table. If the Austrian image was genuine, then the Tennessee picture might be as well. But it is yet another anomaly that stretches our credulity to the limit.

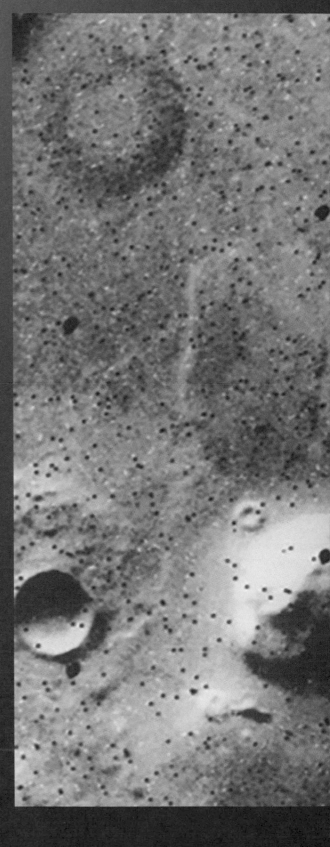

The famous NASA image of the 'Face on Mars' taken on 25 July 1976. Later images have shown its unusual appearance in this photograph to be nothing more than an illusion caused by the play of shadows.

MOVING IMAGES

If just one of the numerous unexplained photographs is genuine, then it follows that we should be able to capture moving images of a phantom. While it is not unreasonable to assume that the majority of clips posted by private individuals on YouTube and other internet sites are crude hoaxes, the same cannot be said about those sourced from surveillance cameras in public places – particularly if that public place is reputed to be haunted.

In December 2003, security cameras at Hampton Court Palace, a London residence of the Tudor king, Henry VIII, recorded an unidentified male figure opening fire doors that the staff had been given strict instructions to keep shut. The man was robed and had an unnaturally white face; no features were discernible when the frames were frozen or enlarged. One of the palace security guards admitted that his co-workers had been spooked because the face 'didn't look human'. Naturally the press suspected it was a publicity prank, but a spokeswoman for Hampton Court Palace fended off the accusation by assuring journalists that staff were just as baffled as everyone else who had seen the footage. 'My first reaction was that someone was having a laugh, so I asked my colleagues to take a look. We spoke to our costumed guides, but they don't own a costume like that worn by the figure. It is actually quite unnerving.'

Ghost hunters were in no doubt that the cameras had caught a genuine manifestation. The palace is reputedly haunted by several spirits. Jane Seymour, Henry's third wife, died there in childbirth and Catherine Howard, Henry's fifth wife, was imprisoned there before her execution at the Tower of London. Their spirits have been seen on numerous occasions, as has that of Sibell Penn, nursemaid to Seymour's son, Edward. Sibell died in 1562 but was disinterred in 1829, after which a strange sound like that of a spinning wheel was heard and traced to the room she had used for spinning.

An image from the 'fire door' sequence was published to much fanfare in periodicals around the world, but not everyone was convinced. Debunkers make the point that the 'spirit' appears unusually solid and seems strangely familiar with the procedure of securing a modern fire door (the safety handle has to be pulled down and the left-hand door must be closed before the right-hand door)! This makes it more likely that one of the guides in period costume was playing a prank. However, to date no one has admitted responsibility for the Hampton Court 'haunting'.

The ghost of Jane Seymour, third wife of Henry VIII, is said to haunt the grounds of Hampton Court Palace.

A RACING CERT

Across the Atlantic in California, a group of paranormal investigators recently recorded a man-sized shadow walking through the bar and exiting through a solid wall at the Del Mar racetrack, a noted haunt of Hollywood celebrities in the 1930s and 1940s. Stars such as Bing Crosby, Mickey Rooney, W.C. Fields and Lucille Ball lived the high life in a private dining club at the track, but the most domineering personality of the era was horse trainer Charlie Whittingham, whose framed photographs still adorn the walls. Numerous witnesses have heard his voice ordering his favourite drink, a martini, and answering their question 'Is anyone there?' with a hearty, disembodied laugh. But his most unnerving appearance was on a night in July 2010, when his shadow was recorded on the paranormal investigators' videotape. As his ghost passes through the wall there is a small flash of light, even though there is nothing but a hall beyond.

Employees have spoken of sensing a cold spot they can measure with their hands when they are feeling brave enough. Some have also seen a small glowing ball floating through the hallways, which then visits each of the guest bedrooms in turn as if searching for something or someone. One or two people have even challenged the celebrity spirits to make their presence known and have been answered with a hoarse laugh or called by name, only to find that they are alone in the room.

The Del Mar racetrack in San Diego, California, is home to a number of celebrity ghosts.

THE SCHOOL SPOOK

On 8 August 2008, surveillance cameras recorded what appeared to be the ghost of a child in Asheville High School, North Carolina, which was closed for the summer vacation. The apparition appears as a shadow on the right of the picture by the elevator, then takes form as it reaches the other side. Even the city schools' spokesman Charlie Glazener, who stated he wasn't a believer in ghosts, told local TV reporters that he didn't have an answer and was now 'one step closer to believing in what we don't normally see'. But one has to ask why a child – dead or otherwise – would choose to go to school when he or she didn't have to, and at three o'clock in the morning!

A ghost of a child was caught on camera during summer vacation in Asheville High School, North Carolina.

OPEN TO DOUBT

It's hard to raise much enthusiasm for a brief clip shot by After Dark Paranormal Investigations, an American organization who set up a camera in an unnamed cemetery and recorded an unusually frisky sprite gambolling in the top right of the frame. While a young, prematurely deceased individual might have returned from the dead to dance among the tombstones, it's too fleeting an appearance to be convincing. Kathy Henley, an employee at Puckett's Car Wrecking Service in Oklahoma City, is convinced that her workplace is haunted by a victim of a fatal crash. In surveillance footage, a white figure can be seen circling the lot. The three vehicles it approaches were all impounded following fatal accidents and Kathy insists that no one could have climbed the security fence and entered the lot without triggering the alarm. But there is a fair chance that another employee was playing a prank on her, so this sighting will have to be filed as 'doubtful'.

GHOSTS OF GETTYSBURG

If you plan to film ghosts but don't live near a castle or haunted house, a battlefield is the next best thing and should be a site worth staking out. Gettysburg, the scene of one of the bloodiest encounters in the American Civil War, has had its share of sightings. In November 2001, a local family saw some lights moving among the trees and decided to investigate. Fortunately, they took a video camera and filmed what they saw. If you are a disbeliever, the short clip won't be enough to convince you, but if you do believe in ghosts, it could freak you out! After a couple of small lights are seen for a second or two, a number of white figures can be glimpsed among the trees in an area of sacred ground that is strictly off-limits to tourists.

The aftermath of the Battle of Gettysburg, 1863. It is hardly surprising that the battlefield has its fair share of ghosts.

SPECTRAL SOLDIERS

During World War I, both the Germans and the Allies reported several sightings of spectral soldiers who intervened to save the lives of their comrades. The most famous was the legendary 'Angels of Mons', which may have been the creation of the English novelist Arthur Machen. However, the following story is generally considered to be authentic. It appeared in the August 1919 issue of the popular *Pearson's Magazine* and was credited to Captain W.E. Newcome.

It was in September, 1916, that the 2nd Suffolks left Loos to go up into the northern sector of Albert. I accompanied them, and whilst in the front line trenches of that sector I, with others, witnessed one of the most remarkable occurrences of the war.

About the end of October, up to November 5th, we were actually holding that part of the line with very few troops. On November 1st the Germans made a very determined attack, doing their utmost to break through. I had occasion to go down to the reserve line, and during my absence the German attack began.

I hurried back to my company with all speed, and arrived in time to give a helping hand in throwing the enemy back to his own line. He never gained a footing in our trenches. The assault was sharp and short, and we had settled down to watch and wait again for his next attack.

We had not long to wait, for we soon saw Germans again coming over No Man's Land in massed waves; but before they reached our wire a white, spiritual figure of a soldier rose from a shell-hole, or out of the ground about one hundred yards on our left, just in front of our wire and between the first line of Germans and ourselves. The spectral figure then slowly walked along our front for a distance of about one thousand yards. Its outline suggested to my mind that of an old pre-war officer, for it appeared to be in a shell coat, with field-service cap on its head. It looked, first, across at the oncoming Germans, then turned its head away and commenced to walk slowly outside our wire along the sector that we were holding.

An illustration of German soldiers encountering the Angels of Mons.

Our SOS signal had been answered by our artillery. Shells and bullets were whistling across No Man's Land . . . but none in any way impeded the spectre's progress. It steadily marched from the left of us till it got to the extreme right of the sector, then it turned its face right full on to us. It seemed to look up and down our trench, and as each Véry light (flare) rose it stood out more prominently. After a brief survey of us it turned sharply to the right and made a bee-line for the German trenches. The Germans scattered back . . . and no more was seen of them that night.

The Angels of Mons seemed to be the first thought of the men; then some said it looked like Lord Kitchener, and others said its face, when turned full on to us, was not unlike Lord Roberts. I know that it gave me personally a great shock, and for some time it was the talk of the company. Its appearance can be vouched for by sergeants and men of my section.

Later in the same article, another officer, William M. Speight, describes seeing the phantom figure in his dug-out that night. The next evening Speight invited another officer to serve as a witness in the hope that the vision might make another appearance. The dead officer duly appeared, pointed to a spot on the floor of the dug-out, then vanished. Intrigued and somewhat superstitious, Speight ordered a hole to be dug at the spot. To the amazement of Speight and the whole company, the sappers unearthed a narrow tunnel that had been excavated by the Germans, primed with mines timed to explode 13 hours later. The timers and explosives were excavated safely and destroyed.

From the numerous accounts of spectral soldiers on file it would seem that fighting men take such sightings in their stride. No doubt frayed nerves, fatigue and the proximity of death play their part in lowering the threshold of awareness which protects ordinary people from glimpsing the world beyond. In his memoirs of World War I, the English poet Robert Graves recalled a sighting which produced only mild curiosity, rather than fear, at the time.

I saw a ghost at Bethune. He was a man called Private Challoner who had been at Lancaster with me and again in F Company at Wrexham. When he went out with a draft to join the First Battalion, he shook my hand and said: 'I'll meet you again in France, sir.' He was killed at Festubert in May and in June he passed by our C Company billet where we were just having a special dinner to celebrate our safe return from Cuinchy . . . Challoner looked in at the window, saluted and passed on. There was no mistaking him or the cap badge he was wearing. There was no Royal Welch battalion billeted within miles of Bethune at the time. I jumped up and looked out of the window, but saw nothing except a fag end smoking on the pavement. Ghosts were numerous in France at the time.

A 'STRANGE MEETING'

One of the finest poets of World War I, Wilfred Owen – who is perhaps best remembered for his atmospheric verse 'Strange Meeting' in which a German and a British soldier encounter each other in the underworld – was killed just one week before the Armistice was declared. On the day the guns finally fell silent, his brother Harold, a naval officer, was overwhelmed by a feeling of apprehension and was later 'visited' in his cabin by Wilfred's spirit. Harold's reaction to the presence of his brother contrasts with the fears of fictional characters who are confronted by unquiet spirits and for that reason his experience is strangely comforting. Harold was unaware of his brother's death at the time of their strange meeting.

I had gone down to my cabin thinking to write some letters. I drew aside the door curtain and stepped inside and to my amazement I saw Wilfred sitting in my chair. I felt shock run through me with appalling force and with it I could feel the blood draining away from my face. I did not rush towards him but walked jerkily into the cabin – all my limbs stiff and slow to respond. I did not sit down but looking at him I spoke quietly: 'Wilfred, how did you get here?' He did not rise and I saw that he was involuntarily immobile, but his eyes which had never left mine were alive with the familiar look of 'trying to make me understand'; when I spoke his whole face broke into his sweetest and most endearing dark smile. I felt no fear – I had not when I first drew my door curtain and saw him there; only exquisite mental pleasure at thus beholding him. All I was conscious of was a sensation of enormous shock and profound astonishment that he

The war poet Wilfred Owen (1893–1918), who was killed just a few days before Armistice Day.

should be here in my cabin. I spoke again, 'Wilfred dear, how can you be here, it is just not possible . . .' But still he did not speak but only smiled his most gentle smile. This not speaking did not now as it had done at first seem strange or even unnatural; it was not only in some inexplicable way perfectly natural but radiated a quality which made his presence with me undeniably right and in no way out of the ordinary. I loved having him there: I could not and did not want to try to understand how he had got there. I was content to accept him, that he was here with me was sufficient. I could not question anything, the meeting in itself was complete and strangely perfect. He was in uniform and I remember thinking how out of place the khaki looked among the cabin furnishings. With this thought I must have turned my eyes away from him; when I looked back my cabin chair was empty . . .

THE CONVERSION OF CONAN DOYLE

Sir Arthur Conan Doyle, creator of the fictional detective Sherlock Holmes, became an enthusiastic advocate of spiritualism in the early days of World War I, much to the dismay of his closest friends and most ardent admirers.

The author and his wife had been nursing a young lady, Lily Loder-Symonds, who was in poor health and spent much of her time practising automatic writing. Doyle was fascinated but had attributed the messages to the action of Lily's subconscious mind until one morning, in May 1915, she declared in some agitation that she had received a warning of impending disaster. 'It is terrible. Terrible. And will have a great influence on the war.' Later that day there came news that the transatlantic liner the *Lusitania* had been sunk by a German submarine with the loss of more than 1,000 lives, 128 of them American. It was the turning point of the war. The Americans were outraged and shortly after entered the war on the side of the Allies.

Doyle began to take an active interest in 'spirit messages' after this and received what he considered to be incontrovertible proof of the soul's survival after death. It came in the form of a 'conversation' with his dead brother-in-law, Malcolm Leckie, who had been killed at Mons in April 1915. Doyle was stunned to witness Lily writing in Malcolm's unmistakable hand and struck up a dialogue during which he asked probing personal questions which only his brother-in-law could have answered, relating to details of a private conversation which they had just before Malcolm returned to the front.

He became an active member of the Society for Psychical Research and attended many séances, including one at which he heard the voice of his son and saw the revenants of his mother and nephew. Galvanized by the experience, he embarked on a worldwide lecture tour to promote the cause. In 1926, he published *The History of Spiritualism*, the result of more than ten years' research into the subject. The book made a convincing case for the existence of psychic phenomena while acknowledging that there were many fake mediums who had no scruples about fleecing the unwary.

Ultimately, Doyle's credibility took a fatal blow after it was revealed that the Cottingley fairy photographs which he had publicly and enthusiastically declared to be genuine were in fact fakes, but his faith in the afterlife remained unshakable until his death in 1930.

Sir Arthur Conan Doyle (1859–1930), best known for his creation Sherlock Holmes, was a keen follower of the spiritualist movement.

Lily's warning of impending disaster: 'It is terrible. Terrible. And will have a great influence on the war.'

THE PHANTOM FAYRE

In October 1916, Edith Olivier turned off the main road to Swindon in Wiltshire, in search of a public house in which she could spend the night and saw ahead the imposing black monoliths which lined the road to the megalithic stone circle at Avebury. Despite the rain she was keen to see the site, which was rumoured to have been the scene of Bacchanalian rituals in pagan times.

She climbed a small mound to get a better view and saw what appeared to be a village fayre in progress. From the sound of the laughter and the applause which greeted the fire eaters, acrobats and jugglers, the villagers were clearly enjoying themselves, undaunted by the weather. But then she noticed something peculiar. The fiery torches they carried were undimmed by the rain and not a single man, woman or child wore a raincoat nor carried an umbrella. It was as if they walked between the raindrops, indifferent to the drizzle which by now was becoming a steady downpour.

Nine years later, when she visited the site again as part of a guided tour, she asked the guide about the fayre. He confirmed that the villagers had held an annual fayre on the site, but the custom had stopped in 1850. It was then that Edith realized that the road approaching the mound she had stood upon was no longer there. The guide agreed that there had been a long dirt road leading to the site in former times, but it had vanished from all maps made after 1800.

MASS MATERIALIZATIONS

While some apparitions appear to be those of earthbound spirits, this explanation cannot account for the many sightings of phantom armies or groups such as the revellers seen by Edith Olivier at Avebury. The conventional theory is that such souls are unaware that they are dead and so continue to relive the drama of their last hours as if trapped in a recurring dream. While this may be true of certain stubbornly persistent personalities, it seems unlikely that hundreds of individual souls would reconvene on the anniversary of their death to relive such an event. What would have compelled the country folk of Avebury, for example, to relive their night at the fayre if there was no tragedy that had entrapped them? It seems more likely that sightings involving a group are an echo across time which can be picked up by anyone possessing heightened perception. In short, the phantoms are not fighting their battles again, the witness is simply tuning into it in their mind and the stronger the emotional residue, the easier it is for one or more people to sense it. If all phantom battles were genuine collective hauntings, most of Europe would echo to ghostly gunfire from dusk to dawn. Why, then, is one battlefield or village the setting for a spectral restaging and not another? Is it because the phantoms are mere ripples in the ether?

The best known example of a mass re-imagining is the phantom battle of Edgehill, which was originally

A re-enactment of a battle from the English Civil War. It is not only the living who enjoy re-enactments – it seems that ghosts are just as keen!

fought on 23 October 1642 between the Royalist Army of King Charles I and the Parliamentary Army commanded by Oliver Cromwell during the English Civil War. So violent was the clash that the ripples were seen and heard by the locals on consecutive weekends two months later.

Naturally, the king was perturbed when he heard rumours that his defeat was being replayed with the same ignominious result so he despatched three of his most loyal officers to see if there was any truth in the tales. They returned ashen-faced to report that not only had they witnessed the re-enactment but that they had recognized several of their friends who had been killed on that day, as well as the king's nephew Prince Rupert, who had survived.

It is tempting to dismiss such tales as the stuff of a more superstitious age, but such phenomena continue to be reported in more modern times. Two English women, holidaying in Dieppe, swore that they heard the sounds of a modern battle just before dawn on the morning of 4 August 1951. The sound of Stuka dive bombers, artillery shells and even the distinctive sound of landing craft hitting the beach was so loud they thought the French army was carrying out a training exercise or perhaps someone was making a war movie. But when they threw open the shutters of their hotel room they saw only empty streets. It was then that they remembered the significance of the date. On the same day nine years previously, a disastrous commando raid cost the lives of almost 1,000 Canadian soldiers.

CHAPTER 3

LIVING APPARITIONS

If we want to understand what a ghost is, we only need to look at living apparitions, which include out-of-body experiences, doppelgängers, crisis apparitions and other ethereal phenomena. After devoting much of his life to paranormal research, Sir Oliver Lodge concluded that ghosts were not conscious entities, but emotional energy recorded in matter.

THE STONE TAPE THEORY

Oliver Lodge's theory of ghosts as emotional energy left behind in matter was to become known as the 'stone tape' theory, and may account for those sightings in which ghosts replay events from the most traumatic moments in their lives, exhibiting no conscious awareness of any witnesses who may be present. According to the hypothesis this type of ghost is merely an echo. But it does not explain the many incidents where apparitions of the living appear in one location while their body resides elsewhere. Neither does it explain how a living apparition can appear carrying an object, unless they have charged that object with their personal energy at the moment they are projecting their etheric body to the second location.

The SPR recorded a typical example of this in which a lady saw her uncle appear in her home carrying a roll of paper. She naturally assumed that he had decided to pay her a visit, but her uncle looked anxious as he strode across the room and out through an open door. By the time she had followed him outside he was nowhere to be seen. Later that day she received a letter from her father

Sir Oliver Joseph Lodge (1851–1940) sought to bring together the transcendental world with the physical universe.

'. . . the many incidents where apparitions of the living appear in one location while their body resides elsewhere'.

informing her that her uncle was gravely ill. He had died at the very same moment he had appeared in her home. As she stood by her uncle's bed, she felt an urge to look under his pillow and there she found a roll of paper on which, she assumed, he had intended to write a new will favouring her or her father.

It seems that the connection between the uncle's spirit and his body were weakening in the final moments of his life and so he was able to project his essence or his thought form to his niece's home. However, there are also well-documented cases of people who were in the best of health when they projected their image many miles away. The most famous example is that of the French schoolteacher Emilie Sagee.

IN TWO PLACES AT ONCE

Miss Sagee was a popular addition to the staff at the Neuwelcke finishing school for young ladies at Livonia (now Latvia) in 1845, but there was something unsettling about her which her pupils could not put into words. She was pretty, capable and conscientious, but at the same time distracted, as if her mind was elsewhere. The trouble was that it was not only her mind that was elsewhere. So was her doppelgänger, her spirit double.

For weeks there had been rumours that Miss Sagee had been seen in two parts of the school at the same time. Naturally, her colleagues scoffed at the very idea and dismissed it as schoolgirl gossip, but they were soon forced to face the fact that there was more to Emilie than met the eye. One of her pupils, Antoine von Wrangel, was unusually anxious the day she prepared for a high society party. Even so, her girlish excitement cannot account for what she thought she saw when she looked over her shoulder to admire herself in the mirror. There, attending to the hem of her dress, was not one but two Mademoiselle Sagees. Not surprisingly the poor girl fainted on the spot. It became no longer a matter of rumour when a class of 13 girls saw Miss Sagee's doppelgänger standing next to its more solid counterpart at the blackboard one day, mimicking the movements of the 'real' Emilie.

However, no one could blame the teacher – she had done nothing improper. By now the whole school was on edge and rife with wild unfounded stories as the girls embellished their experiences for the entertainment of their friends. Eventually, these stories reached the ears of the headmistress, but there were no grounds for a reprimand, never mind a dismissal. Emilie continued to be a conscientious member of staff. The next summer, matters came to a head.

The entire school was assembled one morning in a room overlooking the garden where Miss Sagee could be seen picking flowers. But when the supervising teacher left the room another Miss Sagee appeared in her chair as if from nowhere. Outside, the 'real' Emilie could still be clearly seen gathering flowers, although her movements appeared to be sluggish, as if her vitality had drained away. Two of the more inquisitive girls took the opportunity to step forward and gingerly touch the double in the chair. To one it felt like muslin, but not entirely solid. Another girl passed right through the apparition by walking between the table and the chair. The doppelgänger remained still and lifeless. Moments later it faded and the girls observed that the real Emilie became herself again, moving among the flower beds with some purpose.

The girls quizzed Miss Sagee at the first opportunity, but all she could remember was that when she had seen the teacher leave the room she had wished that she could have been there to supervise the class until their teacher returned. Evidently, her thoughts had preceded her.

Unfortunately for Miss Sagee and the school this incident was not the last. Thirty fee-paying pupils were removed by their concerned parents over the following 18 months after stories about the phenomenon became the prime subject of the girls' letters home. Reluctantly, the headmistress was finally forced to let Miss Sagee go. Emilie was saddened but not surprised. It was the 19th position she had been forced to leave in her 16-year career.

The trouble was that it was not only her mind that was elsewhere. So was her doppelgänger, her spirit double.

THE ABSENT MP

Politicians are not usually considered to be imaginative individuals and so the British newspapers made the most of an incident in 1905 in which the living apparition of British MP Sir Frederick Carne Rasch appeared in the House of Commons at the same moment that his body lay in bed suffering from influenza. Sir Frederick had been so anxious to attend the debate that he had obviously willed himself to appear, but his concentration must have weakened because he vanished before the vote was taken. When he returned to Parliament a few days later MPs delighted in prodding him to see if he was really there in the flesh.

PHANTOM FORERUNNERS

Bi-location may be uncommon, but it is not inconceivable that the mind might be capable of disassociation to such a degree that it enables the essence of a person to appear elsewhere. However, the phenomenon known as the 'phantom forerunner' is far more difficult to explain. The best known example is that of businessman Erkson Gorique, who visited Norway in July 1955 for the first time in his life. Or was it?

When Erkson checked into his hotel the clerk greeted him like a valued customer. 'It's good to have you back, Mr Gorique,' said the clerk. 'But I've never been here before,' Gorique replied. 'You must have mistaken me for someone else.' The clerk was certain he was not mistaken. 'But sir, don't you remember? Just a few months ago you dropped in to make a reservation and said you'd be along about this time in the summer.' Erkson assured the clerk that this was his first visit to the country. The next day he went to introduce himself to his first potential client, a wholesaler named Olsen: 'Ah, Mr Gorique. I'm glad to see you again. Your last visit was much too short.' Erkson was confused and explained what had happened to him at the hotel. To his surprise, Olsen just smiled. 'This is not so unusual here in Norway,' he said. 'In fact, it happens so often we have a name for it. We call it the *vardoger*, or forerunner.'

In England such apparitions have traditionally been filed away as just another inexplicable ghost story. In 1882, Dr George Wyld reported an incident involving a close acquaintance, Miss Jackson. She had been distributing food to the poor in the neighbourhood on a bitterly cold day when she had a sudden urge to return home to warm herself by the kitchen stove. At that moment her two maids were sitting in the kitchen and observed the doorknob turning and the door open, revealing a very lifelike Miss Jackson. Startled at their employer's early return they jumped to their feet and watched as she walked to the stove, took off her green kid gloves and warmed her hands. She then vanished. The maids ran to Miss Jackson's mother and described what they had seen, but the old woman assured them that her daughter did not own a pair of green gloves, so they must have imagined it. Half an hour later the lady herself arrived, walked to the kitchen stove, removed her green kid gloves and warmed her hands.

The Reverend W. Mountford of Boston was visiting a friend when he looked out of the dining room window and saw a carriage approaching the rear of the house. 'Your guests have arrived,' said Mountford, whereupon his host joined him at the window. Both men observed the carriage turn the corner as if it was going to the entrance. But no one rang the doorbell. Instead, the host's niece entered looking rather flustered having walked all the way from her home, and informed Mountford and his host that her parents had just passed her without acknowledging her or offering her a lift.

A ghostly appearance of a horse and carriage preceded the real arrival of the Reverend's guests.

Ten minutes later the real carriage arrived with the host's brother and his wife. They denied all knowledge of having passed their daughter en route.

As recently as 1980 an Austrian woman, Hilda Saxer, reported seeing a grey Audi belonging to her sister's fiancé, Johann Hofer, passing by at 11.30 pm as she left the restaurant where she worked. She waved and the driver, whom she saw clearly and recognized as Johann, smiled and waved back. As she watched the car disappear into the distance the incident struck her as odd because Johann had left the restaurant half an hour earlier. An hour later Johann's father heard his son's car pull into the driveway but he did not hear Johann enter the house. The next morning the radio reported a tunnel collapse on the route Johann had taken on his way home from the restaurant at 11.30 pm that same night. Days later rescuers found the wreckage of the car and its driver, crushed beneath tons of rubble.

CRISIS APPARITIONS

Sailors have always been notoriously fond of a good ghost story, but the tale told by seaman Robert Bruce to the 19th-century paranormal researcher Robert Dale Owen is both singular and significant as it is one of the earliest recorded examples of a crisis apparition, a phenomenon which is more common than one might imagine.

In 1828, Bruce was the first mate aboard a cargo ship ploughing through the icy waters off the Canadian coast. During the voyage he entered the captain's cabin to find a stranger bent over a slate, writing intensely and in great haste. The figure appeared solid, but there was an other-worldly aspect to him and a grave expression on his face which unnerved Bruce.

When the stranger raised his head and looked at him, Bruce fled, fearing that the presence of the phantom foretold disaster for all on board. He found the skipper on deck and persuaded him to return to the cabin. 'I never was a believer in ghosts,' said Bruce as

they made their way below deck, 'but if the truth must be told sir, I'd rather not face it alone.' But when they entered the cabin it was empty. However, they found the slate and on it were scrawled the words 'Steer to the nor'west.'

At first the skipper suspected that the crew were playing a practical joke, so he ordered them all to copy the message. After comparing their handwriting with the original he had to admit he could not identify the culprit. A search of the entire ship failed to find any stowaways, leaving the captain with an unusual dilemma: to ignore the message and risk having the lives of untold lost souls on his conscience, or change his course and risk being thought of as a superstitious old fool in the eyes of the crew. He chose to change course.

Fortunately, he had made the right decision. Within hours they came upon a stricken vessel that had been critically damaged by an iceberg. There were only minutes to save the passengers and crew before it sank beneath the waves. Bruce watched with grim satisfaction and relief as the survivors were brought aboard, but then he saw something which haunted him to his dying day. He came face to face with the stranger he had seen scrawling the message earlier that day in the captain's cabin.

After the man had recovered sufficiently to be questioned, Bruce and the captain asked him to copy the message on the slate. They compared the two sets of handwriting. There was no question about it – they were identical. Initially, the 'stranger' couldn't account for his early presence on the ship until he recalled a dream that he had had about the same time that Bruce had seen his 'ghost' in the captain's cabin. After falling asleep from exhaustion he had dreamt that he was aboard a ship that was coming to rescue him and his fellow survivors. He told the others of his dream to reassure them that help was on its way and he even described the rescue ship, all of which proved correct in every detail. The captain of the wrecked ship confirmed his story. 'He described her appearance and rig,' he told their rescuers, 'and to our utter astonishment, when your vessel hove in sight, she corresponded exactly to his description of her.'

'Within hours they came upon a stricken vessel that had been critically damaged by an iceberg.'

ESCAPING WORLDLY BONDS

One of the most revealing examples of an out-of-body experience was published in a respected medical journal, the *St Louis Medical and Surgical Journal*, in February 1890.

Dr A.S. Wiltse of Kansas contracted typhoid fever in the summer of 1889. After saying his last goodbyes to his family, he lapsed into unconsciousness. But although his body exhibited no signs of life, inside his own dead body, Dr Wiltse was fully conscious and observed the grieving around him with a curious detachment. He then felt a gentle swaying and a separation which he compared to the snapping of tiny cords. In another moment he was looking out from his skull. 'As I emerged from the head I floated up and down . . . like a soap bubble . . . until I at last broke loose from the body and fell lightly to the floor, where I slowly rose and expanded into the full stature of a man.' At this point he felt embarrassed to discover that there were two women in the room, but then he realized that he was not naked but clothed – merely by wishing to be so.

Here, perhaps, is a crucial clue as to why ghosts appear in the form that they do, often younger and in better health than when their physical shell expired. Dr Wiltse had left his body as a shapeless, colourless bubble of etheric energy, but as soon as he became aware of his surroundings he was able to assume a more acceptable form and projected his own idealized self-image. He then passed straight through another man in the room before he realized what he was doing. He saw the funny side of the situation. He intuitively 'knew' that this was his natural state, his true self. He no longer identified with the body on the bed. He was no longer concerned with what happened to it. That was the part of him that felt pain, disappointment, regrets. This 'greater self' was beyond those petty, worldly concerns. If this was 'death', it was nothing more than slipping off a worn-out coat or walking through an open door into the world outside.

He was becoming accustomed to his new 'body'

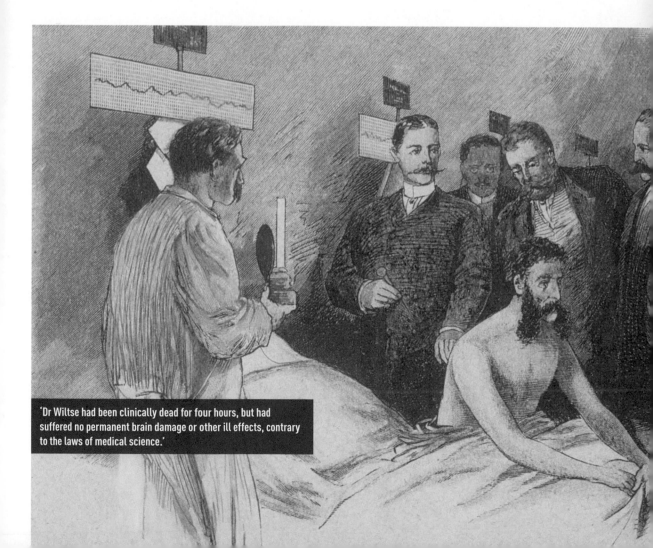

'Dr Wiltse had been clinically dead for four hours, but had suffered no permanent brain damage or other ill effects, contrary to the laws of medical science.'

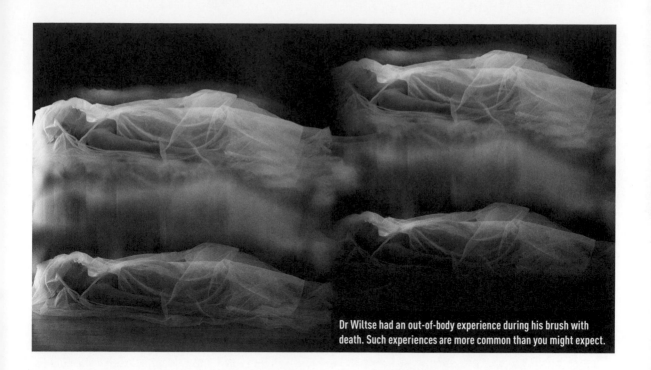

Dr Wiltse had an out-of-body experience during his brush with death. Such experiences are more common than you might expect.

and was eager to explore. As he passed through the door he looked back and saw a thin elasticated web-like cord connecting him to the lifeless body on the bed, the etheric equivalent of the umbilical cord. So long as he remained attached by this cord he knew he could return to his body at will. He was not dead, as he had originally thought, but merely temporarily detached – a living ghost. He walked along a road idly wondering where the other 'dead' people might be and if this is all there was to being dead. Suddenly he lost consciousness and when he next became aware of where he was he found himself in an unfamiliar landscape over which hung a black cloud. Ahead he saw three enormous rocks which an inner voice informed him was the boundary to the 'eternal world'. At this point he intuitively knew that this was as far as he would be permitted to go on this occasion and with that realization he woke up – much to the surprise of his doctor. Dr Wiltse had been clinically dead for four hours, but had suffered no permanent brain damage or other ill effects, contrary to the laws of medical science. A religious man might call this a miracle, but in the years that followed it became increasingly evident that such out-of-body experiences have been shared by hundreds of thousands of people around the world and that they are neither miraculous nor supernatural. They are perfectly natural.

A GHOST IN THE MIRROR

Vermont housewife Caroline Larsen considered herself an unremarkable person, preoccupied with social conventions, her standing in the community and her obligations as the dutiful middle-class wife of an amateur musician. But, one autumn evening in 1910, she discovered her true self as she went one step further than Dr Wiltse had done during a strikingly similar out-of-body experience.

As Mrs Larsen lay in bed listening to her husband and his friends practising a Beethoven string quartet she began to feel a creeping sense of foreboding.

The overpowering oppression deepened and soon numbness crept over me until every muscle became paralyzed . . . Finally everything became a blank. The next thing I knew was that I, I myself, was standing on the floor beside my bed looking down attentively on my own physical body lying in it.

She observed that her room was unchanged. But after heading for the bathroom, she instinctively reached for the light switch and was surprised that she couldn't connect with it. It was then that she noticed that the room was illuminated by a softer light emanating from her own body.

I became aware for the first time of the astonishing transformation I had undergone. Instead of seeing a middle-aged woman, I beheld the figure of a girl about 18 years of age. I recognized the form and features of my girlhood. But I was now infinitely more beautiful. . . I saw, standing before me, a woman spirit in shining clothes with arms outstretched and with forefinger pointing upwards . . . she spoke to me sternly, 'Where are you going? Go back to your body!' . . . I knew instinctively – that from this spirit's command and authority there was no appeal.

Returning to her room she found her body on the bed, just as 'still and lifeless' as she had left it. The image she describes may sound like an aging person's fantasy, but the deceased often appear as their younger selves. In effect, they are so used to having a physical body that they cannot imagine themselves without one and so manifest as their ideal self-image.

The mirror projected back a younger and more beautiful image of the woman.

PROJECTING HIS OWN GHOST

Most of the hundreds of thousands of out-of-body experiences and near-death experiences that have been recorded involve the involuntary separation of the spirit from the body at a moment of crisis or physical danger or during an altered state of consciousness. But there are a surprising number of incidents in which the astral traveller has consciously projected their spirit double to another location.

Sylvan Joseph Muldoon, the son of a spiritualist in Clinton, Iowa, claimed to have acquired the ability to leave his body at will. He had enjoyed dozens of liberating out-of-body experiences since the age of 12, but it was not until ten years later, in 1925, that he had the confirmation that what he was experiencing was more than a lucid dream.

During this excursion he found himself propelled at incredible speed to an unfamiliar farmhouse somewhere in the same rural region where he lived. There he observed four people passing a pleasant evening, including an attractive young girl who was engaged in sewing a black dress. They seemed unaware of his presence so he wandered around the room noting the furnishings and ornaments until it occurred to him that he had no business being there. With that thought he returned to his body. It was more than a month later that Muldoon happened to see the same girl in town and asked her where she lived. She thought he was prying or being 'fresh' and told him to mind his own business, but when he described her home in astonishing detail and told her how he knew this, she confirmed everything that he had seen.

'During this excursion he found himself propelled at incredible speed to an unfamiliar farmhouse somewhere in the same rural region where he lived.'

A MESSAGE FROM THE OTHER SIDE

Near-death experiences typically involve an individual leaving their body, passing through then returning to their body with a renewed appetite for life. But the experience of Dr Karl Novotny was different in one significant respect. He did not return. Instead he described the process of dying from the other side using the services of a medium. Such anecdotal evidence usually has the sceptics shrieking with derision, but the case of Dr Novotny is notable for several reasons.

Two days prior to his death in Easter 1965, Novotny's friend, Grete Schroeder, dreamt that he appeared before her to announce his death. Neither Schroeder nor Novotny were interested in psychic phenomena – in fact quite the reverse. Novotny was a pupil of the celebrated psychologist Alfred Adler and was inclined to explain every phenomenon in terms of the untapped powers of the unconscious. When Novotny died as 'he' had predicted, Grete felt compelled to consult a medium rather than risk becoming prey to doubts for the rest of her life. She evidently chose a reputable psychic because not only did the details of his death – as relayed by the medium – tally with the facts, she also transcribed what he told her in a script which Grete recognized as Novotny's own handwriting even though the medium had never met him. The description of his dying moments is uncannily similar to that related by thousands of other individuals from around the world who have had a near-death experience and it is worth quoting for comparison.

I turned back to my companions and found myself looking down at my own body on the ground. My friends were in despair, calling for a doctor, and trying to get a car to take me home. But I was well and felt no pains. I couldn't understand what had happened. I bent down and felt the heart of the body lying on the ground. Yes – it had ceased to beat – I was dead. But I was still alive! I spoke to my friends, but they neither saw me nor answered me . . .

And then there was my dog, who kept whining pitifully, unable to decide to which of me he should go, for he saw me in two places at once, standing up and lying down on the ground.

When all the formalities were concluded and my body had been put in a coffin, I realized that I must be dead. But I wouldn't acknowledge the fact; for, like my teacher Arthur Adler, I did not believe in after-life.

Novotny then visited his friend Grete and found her sitting alone and immersed in grief, but again his attempts to communicate were fruitless. She did not seem aware of his presence and did not respond when he spoke to her.

It was no use. I had to recognize the truth. When finally I did so I saw my dear mother coming to meet me with open arms, telling me that I had passed into the next world – not in words, of course, since these only belong to the earth. Even so, I couldn't credit her statement and thought I must be dreaming. This belief continued for a long time. I fought against the truth and was most unhappy . . .

Karl Novotny was a student of the psychologist Alfred Adler (left) and not inclined to believe in the presence of ghosts – yet it seems that he became one after his death and continued to communicate with his friend Grete Schroeder.

THE PSYCHOLOGIST AND THE SPIRIT

Dutch psychologist Elleke Van Kraalingen was a pragmatic, scientifically minded woman who prided herself on having a healthy scepticism towards the supernatural. The demands of her professional life meant that she was totally grounded in the here and now and had no desire to probe the secrets of life and death. That was until she witnessed the sudden and violent death of her fiancé, Hermod, in a hit and run accident. In her autobiography, *Love Beyond Death*, Elleke describes how she was awoken to the reality of the soul's survival after death as she knelt over his body and sensed a 'tearing apart' of the subtle bond between them, as it was severed. She then 'saw' his soul leave his body as a mist and sensed his presence standing behind her during her desperate efforts to revive him. After the ambulance had taken his body, Elleke walked back to their hotel, sensing that Hermod was beside her holding her hand.

That evening he materialized in their room, sitting on the edge of her bed as solid as he had been 24 hours earlier. Elleke instinctively denied what she was seeing as a hallucination brought on by grief. She covered her eyes, but when she looked again he was still there and she heard him speak inside her head in a quiet consoling tone. 'I'm still here,' he told her. 'There is no death, there is no time, there's only reality.'

He was not the only discarnate spirit in the room. Elleke sensed the presence of others that she felt were there to help his transition from this world to the next. When he and his companions had gone she wrote everything down so that she could analyze her thought processes at a later date. She hoped this would help her discover the cause of her delusion. Even at this point Elleke was convinced that what she had seen was a projection of her own internal turmoil.

But the next day Hermod reappeared again, as solid as he was when he was alive. Elleke was the only person who could see him, presumably because she perceived him with the eyes of the spirit – the inner eye or third eye of psychic sight. That day he remained with her as she sleepwalked through the traumatic process of identifying his body and dealing with the police. It was only after the funeral that she sensed him withdraw, leaving her to cope with life alone.

Several days later, while Elleke was meditating, he reappeared and drew her out of her body. In this state she was able to look down at her physical self sitting cross-legged on the floor and view the world with a detachment she could not have attained while in her body. She described this state as liberating and more vibrantly real than what she had previously considered to be reality. When they embraced she felt totally absorbed in the core of his being. She sensed that it was only when they were out of body that they could truly know each other. Soon she felt drained and snapped back into her physical shell.

Over the following months, Hermod materialized and took her on an astral tour of other realms or realities where discarnate beings communicated with them by thought alone. In these realms the dead created their own heaven and hell according to their expectations and beliefs. Those who could not accept their own death remained earthbound, reliving the most significant experiences of their lives as if in a recurring dream and visible to the living as ghosts.

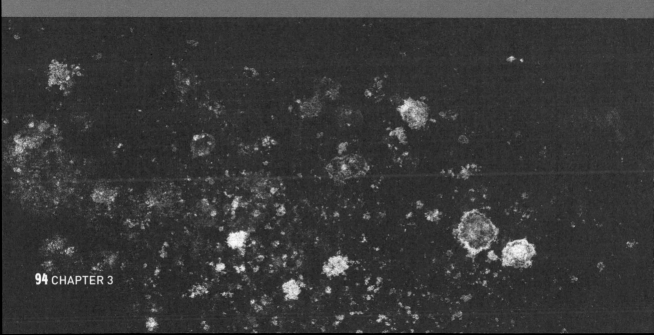

After his death, Hermod reappeared to Elleke several times and gave her a tour of the astral realm.

PSYCHOLOGY AND THE PARANORMAL

Mainstream science and orthodox religion are considered custodians of good sense by those who believe in the infallibility of science or the absolute truth of the Bible. But both fields have their share of individualists who are not as rigid in their thinking.

Carl Jung (1875–1961), the founding father of analytical psychology, was fiercely proud of his reputation as a pioneer of the new science, but in private he continually wrestled to reconcile psychology and the paranormal. Jung's maternal grandfather was said to be blessed with 'second sight'. His family blithely accepted that he conversed with the dead in defiance of Church edicts. His own home life was equally unconventional. As a child Jung was constantly aware of the presence of spirits.

'From the door to my mother's room came a frightening influence. At night Mother was strange and mysterious. One night I saw coming from her door a faintly luminous indefinite figure whose head detached itself from the neck and floated along in front of it, in the air like a little moon.'

In his youth Jung witnessed at first hand phenomena during séances held by his 15-year-old cousin, Helene Preiswerk, who had developed mediumistic powers. Helene channelled a number of dead relatives who spoke in their own distinctive voices and passed on personal details which the young 'Helly' could not have known about. Jung was particularly struck by the change in his cousin's manner when she went into a trance. She exhibited a maturity and breadth of knowledge that was at odds with her provincial frivolous nature. But although Jung was initially convinced that her abilities were genuine, he later felt obliged to find a rational explanation when writing up the case for his inaugural dissertation. It was a classic example of multiple personality, he concluded, brought on by hysteria and sexual repression. Privately, however, he remained a firm believer in the paranormal.

In his autobiography, *Memories, Dreams, Reflections*, Jung describes his own paranormal experiences including the plague of poltergeist activity with which his home was besieged in the summer of 1916.

The house was filled as if it was crammed full of spirits and the air was so thick it was scarcely possible to breathe . . . My eldest daughter saw a white figure pass through her room. My second daughter, independently . . . related that twice in the night her blanket had been snatched away . . .

Over three successive evenings he channelled a series of messages from discarnate spirits which formed the basis of *Seven Sermons To The Dead*, a series of Hermetic discourses on the nature of God, and Good and Evil in a contrived archaic style. It was only when he had completed this task that the spirits withdrew and the 'haunting' ceased. Jung dismissed the attendant poltergeist activity as 'exteriorization phenomena', meaning that he interpreted it as his own unconscious demanding his attention to the coming task.

Helene Preiswerk, cousin of Carl Jung and bona fide medium.

Psychoanalyst Carl Jung (1875–1961) who, together with his teacher and mentor Sigmund Freud, and Alfred Adler, formed the basis of modern psychology and psychotherapy.

THE HAUNTED COTTAGE

Despite a lifetime of witnessing paranormal phenomena at first hand, Jung still felt the need to hedge his bets. In 1919, he wrote a paper for the SPR entitled 'The Psychological Foundation of Belief in Spirits', in which he stated that such phenomena can be dismissed as projections of the unconscious mind. The following year the spirits had their revenge.

In 1920, Jung arrived in Britain on a lecture tour and stayed in a country cottage so that he could be alone. On the first weekend he was disturbed by a rancid odour permeating the bedroom, although there was no obvious source of the smell. The following weekend, the smell returned accompanied by a rustling noise as if an animal was exploring the room, or perhaps a woman in a crinoline dress was brushing against the walls. On the third weekend, his work was interrupted by inexplicable rapping sounds. On the fifth weekend, he was startled to wake up next to the ghost of an old woman, her face partly dissolved as if pressed into a pillow.

The locals subsequently confirmed that the cottage was inhabited by a malevolent spirit and that is why they refused to stay there after dusk. Jung invited the friend who had rented the cottage for him to spend the night, and the man was so terrified when he heard phantom footsteps that he abandoned his bed after just a few hours and spent the rest of the night sleeping in the garden with a shotgun by his side.

His own attitude to such phenomena remained ambiguous despite his extraordinary experiences. He was clearly impressed with the 'performance' of respected medium Rudi Schneider, although he could not bring himself to credit his cousin Helly with the same abilities. For all his insights into the human mind, Jung was forced to admit that he did not have an explanation for these phenomena.

OUT OF THIS WORLD

Paranormal phenomena and psychic experiences pursued Jung all through his life. Then, in April 1944, at the age of 68, he had an out-of-body experience that was to have a profound effect on his perception of the world and which turned his concept of reality on its head. The following extract is from his autobiography, *Memories, Dreams, Reflections* (1961):

It seemed to me that I was high up in space. Far below I saw the globe of the earth, bathed in a gloriously blue light. I saw the deep blue sea and the continents . . . I knew that I was on the point of departing from the earth . . . The sight of the earth from this height was the most glorious thing I had ever seen . . . I myself was floating in space.

At this point Jung felt that he was stripped down to the essence of his being.

. . . everything I aimed at or wished for or thought, the whole phantasmagoria of earthly existence, fell away or was stripped from me – an extremely painful process. . .

When Jung arrived in Britain in 1920, he chose to stay in what appeared to be a cosy country cottage. After a series of unpleasant paranormal encounters, he discovered from locals that it was haunted by a malevolent spirit.

This experience gave me a feeling of extreme poverty, but at the same time of great fullness. There was no longer anything I wanted or desired. I existed in an objective form; I was what I had been and lived.

While he was contemplating the significance of this greater reality he became aware of another presence, that of his doctor who appeared before Jung in his 'primal form'.

In *Synchronicity* (1952), Jung cites the case of a woman patient who left her body during childbirth and observed the medical procedures used to revive her which she described to her nurse after recovering consciousness. She was correct in every detail. The most astonishing part was her discovery that while in her astral body she possessed perceptions independent of her physical senses. At the same moment that she was watching the frantic efforts of the medical staff, she was also aware of a vivid pastoral landscape 'behind' her which she knew to be the 'other world'. By a conscious effort of will she remained focused on the doctors and nurses for fear that she might be tempted by the bliss of the other world to drift into it and not return.

VOICES FROM BEYOND

In the 1920s, Thomas Edison, the prolific American inventor of the phonograph, the electric lamp, the microphone and the kinetoscope (a forerunner of the movie projector), to name but a few of his creations, admitted to working on a device for contacting the dead. He told *Scientific American* magazine that he believed it was perfectly possible 'to construct an apparatus which will be so delicate that if there are personalities in another existence or sphere who wish to get in touch with us in this existence or sphere, this apparatus will at least give them a better opportunity to express themselves than the tilting tables and raps and Ouija boards and mediums and the other crude methods now purported to be the only means of communication.' Unfortunately, Edison passed over before he could build the contraption, but it now seems that his dream may be closer to being realized than ever before.

The first serious hint that audible communication with the departed may be feasible occurred in June 1959 when Swedish ornithologist Friedrich Jurgenson replayed a recording of birdsong and heard a faint Norwegian voice discussing the habits of nocturnal birds. At first he thought it must be interference from a local broadcaster or amateur radio enthusiast, but there was no transmitter in the area. Intrigued, he decided to make test recordings at his home to determine whether or not the tape recorder was faulty, but when he listened to the recordings he caught something which chilled him to the marrow. There were voices on the tape that he had not heard when he was recording. They mentioned Jurgenson and his dog by name and correctly predicted an incoming phone call and the name of the caller. In subsequent recording sessions, Jurgenson merely had to turn on the tape for an unspecified length of time and then play it back to hear a babble of faint voices talking among themselves, commenting on him and the other people whom he had invited to be present as witnesses.

As Jurgenson researched the subject he discovered that EVP (Electronic Voice Phenomena) were only one aspect of a wider range of phenomena known collectively as Instrumental Transcommunication (ITC) covering spirit communication through all manner of electronic equipment including radios, telephones, television sets and even computers. Although the more common forms of ITC are indistinct disembodied voices, there have been incidents where the face of the deceased has been seen and positively identified by their relatives breaking through a regular broadcast on a television screen.

Friedrich Jurgenson heard eerie voices on his tape recordings.

Thomas Edison (1847–1931) in 1928. In 1892, he received a patent for his invention of a two-way telegraph machine, going on to think of designs for a device to contact the dead.

RECORDING EVP

If you want to experiment with EVP all you need is a digital recording device such as a mini-disc, DAT recorder or computer and an analogue radio. Cassette recorders are unsuitable as they produce excessive hiss at low volume and also mechanical noise which can cloak the signal. The radio needs to be tuned to a frequency between stations so that a background of white noise is audible for the voices to print through. You will have to be objective when analyzing what you have recorded as it is possible to interpret random interference, 'print-through' from previous recordings, digital 'artefacts' and signals bleeding from adjacent stations as being significant. The potential for misinterpretation is so strong that a medical term has been coined to describe it – auditory pareidolia. Consequently, it is necessary to remain detached and foster a healthy scepticism, otherwise you are at risk of reading something significant into what is really only random interference.

THE POPE'S PARAPSYCHOLOGISTS

In 1952, two Italian Catholic priests, Father Ernetti and Father Gemelli, were playing back a tape recording they had made of Gregorian chants when they heard an inaudible whispering in the silence when the singing had stopped. At first they thought it might be radio interference or 'print through', the echo of an earlier recording which occurs when the tape has not been properly erased. But when they turned up the volume, Father Gemelli recognized the whispering as the voice of his father who had died many years earlier, calling him by his childhood nickname. 'Zucchini, it is clear, don't you know it is I?'

Contact with the dead is forbidden by the Catholic Church, but there was no denying what they had heard. So the priests dutifully asked for an audience with Pope Pius XII in Rome and put the problem before him. He replied:

Dear Father Gemelli, you really need not worry about this. The existence of this voice is strictly a scientific fact and has nothing to do with spiritism. The recorder is totally objective. It receives and records only sound waves from wherever they come. This experiment may perhaps become the cornerstone for a building for scientific studies which will strengthen people's faith in a hereafter.

The nonchalant reply stunned the priests, but evidently such phenomena were not news to the Vatican. It later transpired that the Pope's cousin, the Reverend Professor Dr Gebhard Frei, co-founder of the Jung Institute, was the president of the International Society for Catholic Parapsychologists.

Before his death in October 1967, Frei had gone on record as a staunch advocate of investigating EVP. 'All that I have read and heard forces me to believe that the voices come from transcendental, individual entities. Whether it suits me or not, I have no right to doubt the reality of the voices.' Just a month after his death, the voice of Dr Frei was caught on tape and identified by Professor Peter Hohenwarter of the University of Vienna.

Pope Paul VI, successor to Pope Pius XII, continued the good work, giving his blessing to researches carried out by Swedish film producer Friedrich Jurgenson, who confided to a British voice researcher in the 1960s, 'I have found a sympathetic ear for the Voice Phenomenon in the Vatican. I have won many wonderful friends among the leading figures in the Holy City.'

The Vatican even agreed to novice priests attending a course in parapsychology under the auspices of Father Andreas Resch. The Church's interest in these phenomena was hardly a secret although it was certainly not widely known. In 1970, the International Society of Catholic Parapsychologists convened in Austria and openly discussed such phenomena as EVP.

Perhaps the Church's most active involvement with such matters was the Pye Recording Studio sessions which took place in England in 1972. The sessions were conducted by theologian Dr Peter Bander, a senior lecturer in Religious and Moral Education at the Cambridge Institute of Education. Prior to the experiment, Bander declared that it was 'not only far-fetched but outrageous' to even consider the possibility of recording spirit voices. He invited four senior members of the Catholic hierarchy to witness the proceedings. But during the recordings, which were held in a soundproof studio to eliminate the possibility of external interference, the participants claimed to hear the voice of a naval officer who had committed suicide two years earlier.

When the *Sunday Mirror* refused to publish Bander's conclusions, he published them himself the following year in a book entitled *Breakthrough*. Father Pistone, Superior of the Society of St Paul in England, gave Bander's experiment and his book a positive endorsement.

Following the publicity surrounding the Pye sessions, the Vatican commissioned Swiss theologian Father Leo Schmid to embark on further research. Schmid went on to amass over 10,000 recordings which were transcribed and edited in his posthumously published book *When the Dead Speak* (1976). It would appear that the Church has made its peace with the dead.

Pope Pius XII was far more open to the idea of paranormal activity than the priests expected.

CHAPTER 4

THE UNINVITED POSSESSION

Claims of haunted possessions are common. Dolls, family heirlooms and even computers might become the subject of a ghostly invasion. But even more unsettling are the cases where a visitor from the spiritual realm decides to take over the mind and body of an unsuspecting victim.

ut now every bargain-hunter sees themself as an amateur antiques expert and every seller prices their bric-a-brac as if they were family heirlooms.

Some shrewd sellers have even come up with a novel method of getting an edge on their competitors in the potentially lucrative online auctions. They claim that their item, be it a doll, a painting or even a games console, is haunted. Many are clearly trying it on, or have their tongues firmly in their cheeks, but to read some of the descriptions and the earnestness with which the seller states their case one has to wonder.

Are the attics and basements of the US and Europe being emptied of genuine possessed possessions? And if so, does the legal term caveat emptor (let the buyer beware) now assume a new meaning?

Arguably the most fascinating and unsettling items on offer are the battered dolls and eerie paintings which must surely give even the most sceptical buyer cause to pause and wonder.

PORTRAIT OF A KILLER?

In 2003 a Florida couple listed a macabre oil painting for sale on eBay entitled *Stricken Life* which was said to have been the work of a murderer who later committed suicide. It was a portrait of an anguished-looking young man smartly dressed in shirt and tie with blood spatter to one side of the canvas and the spookiest part of the matter, say the owners, is that a second face can be seen in the blood and it's screaming!

On the reverse was attached an equally unsettling self-penned poem:

Scraping the sides, running then slowing to a crawl-reajusting (sic) the pace numerous times reaping and sowing this rotten crop. Traffic signs leading me to the messia (sic) of red lights. Struck by a notion to bury the living and save the dead. . .

Knowing that many would laugh into their laptops at such a loopy story the buyers added a lengthy description, explaining how the painting came to be in their possession and assuring potential bidders that they would provide a complete provenance with the work, 'including signed and NOTORIZED depositions by my wife and I, a local publication's account of the night of the murder-suicide, a copy of the release we had to sign before we could purchase the house, ALL pertinent

names and information, as well as anything else we can come up with that pertains to this subject.'

They claim that it was one of the items left behind by the former owner of their new home, which they had purchased at a greatly reduced price because it was rumoured to be haunted. He was the son of a Cuban national who had lived in the house since the mid-1970s. The only other facts that they knew about him, or that they were prepared to divulge online, was that his name was Harold, he had been born in 1949 and he killed his bedridden wife with a shotgun after he had been diagnosed with brain cancer and would not be able to look after her. The sellers take up the story:

Our initial thought was to get rid of the painting, but our teenage son thought it was 'cool'. So on the wall it went, along with an interesting story for our friends. Then the strange sounds in the night started. Always in the night, when it was the darkest. My wife and I were in the master bedroom. It was after midnight, and it was our third night in the new house. I had just dozed off when BOOOM!!! the explosive sound of a shotgun blast jerked me awake. SERIOUSLY. My heart about to explode out of my chest, I sat up in bed. My wife still slept. After securing the house, I came back to bed, thinking it was a dream. Several hours later I was awakened again by the most ungodly howling I had ever heard.

This was their dog. When the husband went to see what was troubling it he found the dog howling at the painting. Disturbed and unable to sleep, he took the painting down and locked it in a closet. Then a couple of nights later his wife woke screaming. She said she had seen a woman in a wheelchair at the end of the bed. But there was no sign of her when the husband finally rubbed the sleep out of his eyes. Then the electrical problems began.

Every bulb in a chandelier in their living room burst, the TV would turn itself on and a woman's voice could be heard calling from the master bedroom.

It was then that they decided to list the portrait on eBay, the only picture 'Harold' is thought to have painted. The whereabouts of the painting are not known and the successful bidder's name has never been disclosed, but the former owners should be getting a good night's sleep from now on.

THE HAUNTED EBAY PAINTING

Haunted paintings have been the subject of several traditional Victorian ghost stories in which the main protagonist becomes transfixed by a picture which appears to have a life of its own. Whenever the owner returns to admire his purchase he is convinced that the figures have moved. Darren Kyle O'Neill told the remarkable story of one such occurrence in his book *The Hands Resist Him: Be Careful What You Bid For* (2016). When buyers saw a painting advertised as haunted on online auction house eBay in February 2000, many must have thought it was a joke. But the anonymous owners, a couple from California, had the last laugh

when it sold for over a thousand dollars. The question that remains unanswered though, is whether this was a genuine paranormal artefact, or merely a clever sales pitch. The picture depicted two children and, although there was very little remarkable in the subject or the manner in which it was painted, the seller claimed in their sales pitch that it possessed a distinctly singular quality:

One morning our 4-year-old daughter claimed that the children in the picture were fighting and coming into the room at night. Now, I don't believe in UFOs or in Elvis being alive, but my husband was alarmed. To my amuseument, he set up a motion-triggered camera for the night. After three nights there were pictures. After seeing the boy seemingly exiting the painting under threat we decided that the painting had to go.

The only clue to the origin of the mysterious picture, which is thought to date from the mid-1960s to the mid-1970s, are the words *The Hands Resist Him* inscribed in pencil across the back.

The sellers felt it necessary to add a disclaimer, either to indemnify themselves against possible future litigation in the event of supernatural phenomena or perhaps to make it more appealing. This was sufficient to encourage a flurry of inquiries which seems to have set the sellers on the defensive. But several potential purchasers reported that the power of the painting extended to their own computers after viewing it online.

'Seven emails reported strange or irregular events taking place when viewing this image,' the seller reported after the sale had closed, 'and I will relay two suggestions made by the senders. First, not to use this image as the background on [your] screen and second, not to display this image around juveniles or children.'

The Hands Resist Him, a disquieting title for an unsettling painting.

GHOST IN A BOTTLE

Without doubt the most unusual spooked item to be listed online has to be the 'ghost in a bottle' auctioned on eBay in December 2004 which a national newspaper claimed had aroused the interest of an agent representing the singer Michael Jackson. Whether Jackson put in the winning bid is not known as the buyer's identity was never revealed.

The bottle was the property of retired mill worker John McMenamin from Spamount, County Tyrone, Northern Ireland, who discovered it cemented into a bricked-up window of their reputedly haunted mill house, but held on to it for 25 years before deciding to cash in.

It was described as being at least a hundred years old and said to contain the imprisoned spirit of a ruthless landlord who had committed suicide after getting a young girl pregnant and then abandoning her to her fate. Angry locals then hounded him to his death. Apparently a local priest had failed to exorcize the ghost from the house, but had managed to force it into the bottle, presumably by promising the disembodied drunkard that stronger spirits awaited him in the bottom of the bottle.

Incredibly, the story caught the imagination of a Northern Irish radio presenter who tracked down and interviewed McMenamin's sister, Marie Maguire, who told the listeners that the bottle contains black dust and is sealed with a page of the Bible. She revealed that when her family moved into the house they knew it was haunted – indeed, that was why the previous occupants left. Maguire went on to describe childhood experiences, including 'waking up, screaming that somebody was looking at me in bed'. Her brother had reported something coming up the bed 'like a cat's paws'. She concluded by saying that the family wanted the purchaser to treat this 'genuine Irish ghost in a bottle with respect'.

VOODOO DOLLS

There are now so many 'haunted dolls' for sale on eBay that they have their own listings category. Some dealers specialize in these novelties and curiosities which vary from battered, blank-eyed babies that would send any kiddie screaming to its mummy, to sweet old lady dolls designed to serve as surrogate grannies. Some sellers claim that they created their dolls to capture the spirit of a loved one or a friendly ghost which they now offer

A bottle supposedly containing a ghost attracted great attention when it was put up for sale on eBay.

as house guests for those in need of companionship or protection. But even the cutest come with a warning that they are not to be given to children or people of a nervous and imaginative disposition. The following is typical of those on offer.

According to this seller her dolls become animated after dark, talking and laughing with each other, which the new owners might find unsettling if they are not prepared for it. She claims to have captured the secret life of the dolls on infrared video and EVP recordings (ethereal sounds beyond the range of the human ear). The pride of her collection contains the spirit of a 92-year-old widow named 'Granny' for whom she provides a biography. The old lady was said to be a kindly 'wise woman' who kept a garden to raise vegetables to feed the needy and herbs to cure ailments until she was cruelly murdered by an intruder.

After her death the seller's grandmother and an aunt who was a medium made the doll in the old lady's image right down to the moles on her face and a miniature copy of her wedding ring. Her clothes too were copied from those she had worn on the last day of her life. Revealingly, no mention is made of the method by which the spirit was summoned and bound in the doll's body, but we do get a list of Granny's likes and dislikes and of her nocturnal activities.

There are a wide range of haunted dolls around, from friendly ghosts of passed loved ones to cruel and dangerous spirits.

THE DIBBUK BOX

The whole subject of 'haunted' possessions invites a healthy dose of scepticism, but one item in particular has attracted a great deal of attention.

In September 2001 a house clearance sale in Portland, Oregon included a box containing an evil spirit known in Jewish mythology as a 'Dibbuk'. The former owner was supposedly an elderly Jewish immigrant who had been the sole surviving member of her family to be liberated from a Nazi concentration camp in Poland. She emigrated to America with her only remaining possessions – a small trunk, a sewing case and the Dibbuk box.

Her granddaughter organized the sale and confided that the old lady had kept it locked and out of the reach of curious children. When asked what it contained, she would spit three times through her fingers and mumble something about a 'Dibbuk' and 'keselim'. Her dying wish was that the box should be buried with her, but orthodox Jewish tradition forbade that, so it was included in the sale.

It was listed as an antique wooden wine cabinet, although one of its subsequent owners has speculated that it was too small to contain wine bottles and glasses would not fit in the rack. However, it may have had a perfectly innocent origin as a liquor cabinet in which could be stored a decanter, shot glasses and tumblers. Inside were two pennies dated 1928 and 1925, two locks of hair bound with string (one fair and one dark), a small statuette engraved with the Hebrew word SHALOM (peace), one dried rosebud, a golden wine cup and a black cast-iron candlestick holder with octopus legs.

The buyer stored it in the basement of his furniture store. He soon became uncomfortable in its presence and decided to sell it on. Apparently, all nine bulbs in the basement and ten fluorescent strip lights had blown simultaneously. His female assistant had been reduced to a gibbering wreck by 'something' that she had seen and which had locked her in while he had been away.

Two weeks later he examined the box more closely and discovered an inscription on the back which he later learned was a Jewish prayer of consecration and protection. When he presented his mother with the refurbished cabinet as a birthday present she seemed pleased, but within minutes she suffered a stroke which left her partially paralysed. The only means she had of communicating was to write shakily and the message she scrawled was anything but reassuring: 'H-A-T-E-G-I-F-T'.

It was then sold through eBay to a young man who began to suffer recurring nightmares of being attacked by an old hag. When he gave it to his sister and brother-in-law, they returned it complaining of having a strikingly similar dream. The young man in turn sold it to a middle-aged couple who left it on his doorstep soon after without asking for their money back.

Bad luck seemed to plague him from that day on. The lease on his store was terminated without explanation and all the fish in his aquarium died. While researching the legend of the Dibbuk he fell asleep at his computer and awoke to feel something breathing down his neck.

The box may have been connected with a Jewish lady who emigrated from Poland around the time of Kristallnacht (the night of broken glass).

THE HISTORY OF THE BOX

In February 2004 the box was acquired for $280 by its present owner, who made great efforts to learn its history. The artefacts such as the braids of hair and the pennies were part of the charms that would bind it in the box. But the ritual did not go according to plan and although the entity was eventually subdued it managed to reap destruction on a scale unprecedented until that time. On 10 November 1938, the Nazis unleashed Kristallnacht (the night of broken glass) when their thugs burnt synagogues throughout Germany and smashed the windows of Jewish-owned shops and businesses.

GHOST IN THE MACHINE

Who can safely scoff and say that the next time their computer crashes while they are online it isn't because they have inadvertently downloaded a cyber spook? Be very careful the next time you curse your computer – you may be invoking an evil spirit!

We have all damned our computers when they freeze up or crash losing valuable data, but we don't seriously believe that our PCs are possessed. But there are frustrated users who would swear on a stack of Bibles that their hard drive is haunted.

Down south in God's own country, Savannah, Georgia, the Reverend Jim Peasboro regularly takes to his pulpit to preach against that spawn of Satan, the World Wide Web. He warns of how computers have 'opened yet another door through which Lucifer and his minions can enter and corrupt men's souls'.

Peasboro contends that PCs have enough storage capacity to house evil spirits, and that members of his congregation have come into contact with a 'dark force' when they have used their computers.

He tells of how happily married men have been drawn to pornographic websites and 'forced to witness unspeakable abominations'.

Some might argue that it is not Satan who forces these men to explore their dark side but human nature, and that Satan is merely a convenient excuse for them to absolve themselves of the responsibility for their actions.

But it's not only men apparently who have been tempted off the straight and narrow, from the path of righteousness. According to the minister, even God-fearing Christian women felt compelled to visit online chat rooms which have turned them from desperate housewives into foul-mouthed, fornicating sinners.

The minister tells of how one woman wept as she confessed to a feeling of being 'taken over' when online. In this particular case the crusading preacher took it upon himself to fight the good fight.

He visited the woman's house, where the computer 'talked to and openly mocked' him. It even typed by itself, calling Peasboro a 'weakling' and told him that 'your God is a damn liar'.

Then without being instructed it spewed out pages of doggerel, an experience that most of us will be familiar with. But the minister is adamant this was not a simple malfunction. He claimed to have had an expert in dead languages examine the text. The expert asserted it to be a 'stream of obscenities written in a 2,800-year-old Mesopotamian dialect'!

Reverend Peasboro is also confident that many school shootings like the tragedy at Columbine were perpetrated by computer buffs, having 'no doubt that computer demons exerted an influence on them'.

So what is to be done about this invasion? Is exorcism the only answer? According to the Reverend Peasboro there is a less drastic solution.

'Technicians can replace the hard drive and reinstall the software,' he says with confidence, 'getting rid of the wicked spirit permanently.'

Amen to that.

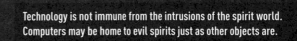
Technology is not immune from the intrusions of the spirit world. Computers may be home to evil spirits just as other objects are.

PHANTOM PHONE CALLS

If it is true that ghosts are merely the discarnate spirits of the living and that they possess the same personality that they had in life, then it is to be expected that the recently deceased would try to communicate with us using the telephone or even email rather than by table-rapping and ectoplasmic manifestations favoured by Victorian spooks.

Julia K's 5-year-old son had shown no interest in the family phone until one day when he stopped playing to answer it. Only it wasn't ringing. At least his mother couldn't hear anything. The child picked up the receiver and entered into a lively conversation, then paused to pass the receiver to his mother who was in the kitchen preparing dinner.

'Who is it?' she asked him, wondering if it could have rung while she was too distracted to hear it.

'Grandmom,' he answered.

'What does she want?'

'She wants to talk to you. She wants to say goodbye.'

His mother took the phone, and anxiously put it to her ear, but she heard nothing. She was relieved and uneasy at the same time. Her mother had died five years earlier and she had never talked about the old lady to her son because she felt he was too young to understand about death. He had not even mentioned her name until that moment.

There was no mistaking the voice on the other end of the line which woke 'Michelle' one Sunday morning. It was her father who she describes as having a great bear of a voice like the actor James Earl Jones who lent his voice to Darth Vader in the Star Wars films. She was recovering from surgery at the time and he began by asking how she was feeling. He also inquired whether she had heard of the death of two people they knew, but she hadn't. At least, not yet. Before he hung up he assured her that life would improve for her and told her that she was not to allow the illness to sap her strength or her spirits. 'When I hung up the phone, it was as if I

Sometimes ghosts do not appear in any visible form, but nonetheless are fully capable of using modern means of communication. Several people have reported holding conversations with the deceased over the phone.

stepped from another level back into this one,' she later wrote. The call had occurred on 13 September – the second anniversary of his death.

COLD CALLING

The following incident sounds like an urban legend, but Terrie, the young lady who reported it to about.com, insists she experienced this herself while working as a temp for an American telemarketing firm.

Telemarketing calls are commonly made by a computer so the salespeople don't have to dial, but if and when the call is answered they have a scripted sales pitch taped to the desk which they are trained to run through before the caller has a chance to hang up. On this particular occasion an elderly man answered and listened patiently while Terrie went through her prepared speech. When she had finished he asked her how much it was going to cost because he and his wife were on social security and had to be careful what they spent.

But as soon as Terrie started to explain she was interrupted by an old woman who called out 'Hello?' Terrie explained that she was talking to Mr Smith to which the woman replied, 'Miss, I'm sorry, Mr Smith has been gone for three years now. He passed away.'

Unperturbed, Terrie asked, 'Is there someone else there I could have been talking to?' to which the old lady replied, 'No, honey. I'm here by myself. Can I help you with something?'

Terrie must have looked as white as a sheet when she hung up because the following day her supervisor pulled the call logs and dialled the number in case an intruder had answered the phone. But the old woman assured the supervisor that she was alone in the house and she was well.

In fact, it took some time before she was convinced that the salespeople weren't pulling her leg about the old man.

POLTERGEISTS

The word poltergeist derives from the German name for a 'noisy ghost', but there is compelling evidence to suggest that in many cases the 'victims' are unconsciously practising a form of psychokinesis, in which an excess of unchannelled mental energy is discharged into the atmosphere affecting electrical equipment and even moving small objects.

That, of course, leaves a number of incidents for which there can be little doubt that a malevolent entity was responsible for the often violent assaults and other disturbing phenomena.

THE ROSENHEIM CASE

In one of the most remarkable incidents of poltergeist activity on record the disturbances were attributed to an 18-year-old girl whose neurotic disposition is thought to have triggered what amounted to a psychic temper tantrum.

In November 1967 Sigmund Adam, a Munich solicitor, was becoming concerned about a number of electrical faults in his office which were threatening to disrupt his business. He was having to buy new fluorescent strip lights every few days when they should have lasted months and the electric meter had registered inexplicable surges of current which also added to his bill.

The electricians he called in were baffled. During tests their voltmeters registered 3 volts when connected to a 1.5 volt battery which indicated that there was another source of power leaking into the atmosphere. Such a thing was simply impossible. On Adam's insistence the lighting company installed a generator in case the fault was in the power lines and they advised Adam to use bulbs in place of the strip lights. But the power surges continued and the bulbs blew with monotonous regularity. The generator was replaced, but the problems persisted. Then other phenomena began to occur. The next telephone bill that Adam received listed dozens of calls every day to the speaking clock. None of the staff admitted to making the calls and

Munich solicitor Sigmund Adam was becoming concerned about the number of electrical faults in his office.

besides, the speaking clock was being dialled up to six times a minute which was impossible as it took at least 17 seconds to dial the number and be put through. Before Adam could figure that one out, the office was besieged by more 'conventional' poltergeist activity. On several occasions a heavy filing cabinet moved of its own accord and pictures spun on the wall as if turned by unseen hands.

Rumours of the disturbances attracted the attention of the national newspapers and as a result of the publicity Professor Hans Bender of the Institute of Paranormal Research at Freiburg offered to investigate. Bender soon discovered that the disturbances only occurred when clerk Ann-Marie Schaberl was present. He also learnt that the ceiling lights were seen to swing whenever she walked underneath them. Under questioning, Ann-Marie admitted that she had watched the speaking clock obsessively as she was so bored. It was Bender's contention that she was unconsciously generating psychokinetic energy to an abnormal degree due to her frustration and, as if to prove his theory, the activity abruptly ceased when she left the office.

Bender concluded that Ann-Marie's intense, neurotic personality had manifested in certain paranormal phenomena and he wondered if it meant that she might possess other psychic abilities which could be scrutinized under laboratory conditions. In the initial tests she showed no signs of such talents, but after the professor raised the subject of a traumatic illness she had suffered for a whole year her scores increased dramatically.

When she returned to Adam's office the activity resumed, forcing him to dispense with her services. Similar disturbances occurred at her next two jobs with apparently tragic consequences. Ann-Marie was blamed for a colleague's death by the other members of staff, although there was no evidence to support their suspicions and she was forced to move on. Things deteriorated further when her fiancé broke off their engagement, complaining that every time he took her bowling the electronic scoring system would malfunction. It was only after she met and married another man and settled down to raise a family that the phenomena ceased and Ann-Marie was left in peace.

THE PONTEFRACT POLTERGEIST

A large proportion of poltergeist activity may be attributable to surges of psychokinetic energy and in rare incidents, possibly to the unconscious creation of thought forms, but there are several well-documented cases which appear to offer compelling proof of the presence of malevolent spirits.

In 1966 the Pritchards of Pontefract, Yorkshire were a typical middle-class British family. Mr Pritchard had a good, steady job which allowed his wife Jean to stay at home to look after their two children, 14-year-old Diane and 5-year-old Philip. But their safe suburban life was soon to be violently disrupted. It began innocuously enough with pools of water on the kitchen floor. Both children furiously denied having played a prank. They weren't aware at the time that the unexplained appearance of water on walls and floors is a characteristic feature of a poltergeist attack.

When more pools appeared the water board inspectors were called in, but they could find no trace of a leak. They had two years of normality before the phenomena returned, this time centring on Diane.

Loud reports accompanied the smashing of crockery and other ornaments. So loud were these noises that neighbours would gather outside the house and wonder if the normally placid couple were having an all-out domestic spat. The children told their friends that Diane had been dragged out of bed by unseen hands and the parents confided to the neighbours that she had been pinned to the floor on several occasions by falling furniture.

When she turned she found herself confronting a tall hooded monk whose face was hidden by a cowl.

Curiously, despite the damage it caused, all this activity never actually hurt anyone. Only at the end did the spirit turn nasty, dragging Diane up the stairs in full view of her father, mother and brother who tackled the unseen entity, forcing it to loosen its grip on her throat. But in case anyone thought this was the girl's attempt to get attention, she was able to show them a set of angry red fingermarks on her neck. And Diane's mother confirmed her story, adding that she had seen large footprints at the bottom of the stairs that day and that the carpet had been soaking wet.

The poltergeist was evidently not content with being a nuisance. Soon after the attack on Diane it decided to scare the family to death by manifesting in the form of a hooded monk. Mr and Mrs Pritchard described seeing a spectral figure in the night framed in an open doorway and

several independent witnesses saw shadowy glimpses of what appeared to be a hooded figure in black elsewhere in the house. On one occasion a neighbour claimed to have felt a distinctive presence behind her and when she turned around found herself confronting a tall hooded monk whose face was hidden by a cowl. An instant later it disappeared. The final sighting occurred one evening when Mr and Mrs Pritchard saw a tall silhouette darken the frosted glass of the dining room door. When they looked inside the room they saw a shadowy shape sink slowly into the floor. It was the last incident in the baffling Pontefract case.

Subsequent research has unearthed the fact that the Pritchard house had been built on the site of a gallows where a Cluniac monk had been hanged for rape during the reign of Henry VIII.

THE PYROMANIAC POLTERGEIST

The standard explanation for all poltergeist activity is that it is caused by displaced energy emitting from an emotionally volatile member of the household, usually an adolescent in the midst of puberty. But this cannot account for the life-threatening disturbances that plagued the Gallo family of Orland Hills, Chicago in the spring and summer of 1988.

It was Dina, one of the couple's two teenage daughters, who first became aware that there might be a phantom firebug in their home when she noticed a shower of sparks from an electrical outlet which quickly set a pair of curtains ablaze. She managed to smother the fire before it could take hold and then she called the fire department, but they failed to find a fault. The only clue Dina could offer was the fact that she had heard a strange popping sound seconds before the sparks appeared. They were soon to realize that it had not been a freak accident. Something was seriously wrong in the Gallo residence.

A more serious fire began in an empty room and inexplicably extinguished itself before the family could race to the scene, leaving scorched drapes, a blackened carpet and the room full of smoke. The next mysterious blaze began in an unoccupied upstairs room and consumed a desk and another set of curtains. Again, the fire department could find no logical explanation for the fire. Why, they wondered, had several objects near to the source of the flames escaped scorching while the desk had not? To reassure them and get to the bottom of the mystery, the fire department called in electrical engineers to check out the wiring and the outside cables in. But it all seemed in order, except for the fact that even after the power had been cut off and all appliances had been pulled out, several sockets started to emit choking smoke.

It was clear that the entire wiring set-up would have to be ripped out and replaced. It was a costly and disruptive cure, but even this did not solve the problem. Now the new sockets emitted sparks. It was at this point that several members of the investigation team began to talk of seeing a white fog of sulphurous fumes which gave them throbbing headaches. But when they brought in sophisticated equipment to measure the levels of carbon monoxide and other poisonous fumes the meters failed to register gas of any kind.

Then on 7 April the sulphurous cloud appeared again, this time in plain sight of several family members who witnessed a long blue flame shooting out of one outlet and scorch marks appearing around others. The climax of this particular display was the spontaneous incineration of a mattress which was later inspected by experts who estimated that the heat which consumed it must have been in excess of 1,500 degrees Fahrenheit (816 degrees Celsius).

The Gallos were desperate. Reluctantly they agreed to pay for the demolition of the house and the building of a new home from scratch.

The story was picked up by the local media, who repeated rumours that fire investigators had consulted psychics and that they had confirmed that the house had been built on the site of three unknown graves. There was also speculation centring on the Gallos' daughter Dina who, it was said, was always in close proximity to the fires. The phenomenon did die down after Dina grew out of her teens, but surely even the most emotional adolescent could not cause the appearance of two-feet-high flames and thick miasmas of sulphurous fog.

Most of us enjoy being frightened by tales of hauntings, possessions and poltergeists in the safety of a cinema, or while curled up in an armchair reading a novel. But what is it like to experience these horrors for real? If the claims of Connecticut housewife Denice Jones are to be believed any family can be caught up in these living nightmares.

Her son Michael had a troubled birth and it was touch and go whether he would survive. During those crucial first weeks of his life he was declared technically dead on more than one occasion. Denice thinks that he crossed over and returned so many times that when he came back he 'left a door open' to the next world. Denice is convinced that her younger son Michael inherited this 'gift' as a direct result of his early brushes with death.

It was not long before the family moved into a new house that they realised that something was seriously wrong. Denice was working in the garden when she heard a piercing scream. Rushing up to Michael's room, she saw him cowering in the corner muttering something about an old man who had appeared from nowhere and touched him on the shoulder.

The Jones family were not the only people to be taunted by the entities in their home. When Denice's sister and her children came to stay with them, Denice's young niece ran screaming from the bathroom. Something had turned the water full on in the hand basin and was laughing at her. The children and their mother refused to stay in the house a moment longer.

Then the growling began. It was an ominous, threatening sound which couldn't be traced to any specific spot. That's what made it so unnerving.

As the attacks on Michael intensified, leaving him in a paralysed state for anything between two and six hours, Denice was forced to take him out of school and educate him at home. Life for the whole family was becoming intolerable. The children wouldn't go to the bathroom or even fetch a snack alone. Even Denice was afraid to stay in the house by herself – she would sit in her car in the parking lot until it was time to collect the kids.

Eventually they turned to a team of paranormal investigators for help. The investigators captured EVP (electronic voice phenomena) and what Denice refers to as 'abnormalities' in several photographs that they took. Eventually their relationship degenerated to the point

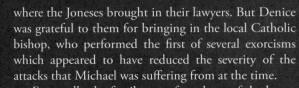

where the Joneses brought in their lawyers. But Denice was grateful to them for bringing in the local Catholic bishop, who performed the first of several exorcisms which appeared to have reduced the severity of the attacks that Michael was suffering from at the time.

Eventually the family were forced out of the house by the relentless poltergeist activity.

EXORCISTS

If ghosts are either residual personal energy echoing in the ether or discarnate earthbound spirits and poltergeist phenomena can be attributable mainly to involuntary bursts of telekinetic energy, is there any compelling evidence for belief in the existence of evil spirits? Or are the cases of demonic possession a symptom of ingrained superstition and the misdiagnosis of serious personality disorders?

DEMONS AND DEVILS

The date 11 December 1937 was as infamous as any in the history of warfare for it was the date of the atrocious massacre at Nanking. Hundreds of thousands of innocent Chinese civilians were butchered by invading Japanese troops who were running amok. It was a scene of hell on earth, but in the midst of the carnage and chaos the gates of the underworld were gaping wide for a real demon, a cannibalistic serial killer who had been tracked down to his hideout in a disused grain store. The police had surrounded the building and were determined to see justice done.

But this was no ordinary criminal case. Father Michael Strong, the local parish priest, asked them to delay the arrest while he conducted an exorcism. It was his belief that the fugitive, Thomas Wu, had murdered and eaten his victims while possessed by a demon and he was going to drive it out.

When the police captain arrived on the scene, he found Father Michael standing over the cowering naked figure of Thomas Wu, who brandished a knife in one hand. He was in a severely agitated state and looked like a cornered animal who might spring out of his lair at any moment. Arranged around the walls on wide wooden shelves were the decaying corpses of dozens of Wu's victims. What kind of man could have perpetrated these atrocities? But it was not a man. It was a demon and he was about to reveal his true face, or faces, for the astonished onlookers.

'YOU!' screamed Wu in a voice both the captain and the priest did not recognize even though they had known him since he had been a boy. 'YOU want to know MY name!'

At this outburst Father Michael staggered backwards as if the force of the words had dealt him a body blow. Father Michael's exhortations in the name of Jesus had no effect on the grinning, slavering man who seemed to summon up inhuman reserves of strength to draw

The infamous massacre of Nanking which took place in 1937, but it was not just the Japanese who were slaying citizens.

A Ouija board is an effective way of communicating with the spirit world.

himself up to his full height and bellow like some wounded beast. 'Get out of here. Get the hell out of here, you filthy old eunuch!'

It took all of Father Michael's faith to remain upright and, his voice shaking with emotion, continue to demand that the unclean spirit depart.

Wu roared a string of expletives at the beleaguered priest which were suddenly cut short when the roof timbers caught alight. The next instant the police captain had grabbed Father Michael and was pulling him from the burning building.

From just a few feet away they watched the flames consume the wooden grain store together with their quarry and the mutilated bodies of his victims. But Thomas Wu did not go quietly and neither did the spirit which possessed him. A face appeared at the window, a hideous, contorted face which Father Michael later described as having 'the thumbprint of Cain' upon it. From within they heard a hideous mocking laugh and then they witnessed a shocking sight. Wu's features dissolved and in its place a succession of faces appeared as if the demon's former hosts were being released in Wu's death agony. They were the half-remembered faces

of Father Michael's nightmares. Others he thought he had seen in old churches. Some were male, some female. They were of every race and nationality, but they shared one characteristic. They were all evil. Then the window went black and the wooden structure collapsed in a sheet of flame and smoke.

Such a scene might sound like a script from a horror movie, but this event is said to be as true as the massacre of Nanking and not untypical of the confrontations experienced by real exorcists who claim to be fighting the good fight to this day.

THE EXORCIST

Author Peter Blatty based his bestselling novel *The Exorcist* (which became the basis for the controversial film of the same name) on a real case of alleged demonic possession which had occurred in a suburb of Washington DC in the first four months of 1949. According to a report in the *Washington Post* that year, a 14-year-old boy by the name of Robbie Mannheim had exhibited classic symptoms of possession, specifically spontaneous body wounds, involuntary bouts of abusive language and a distinct change of personality after trying to communicate with the spirit world using a Ouija board. Doctors who examined Robbie could find no medical reason for his behaviour, or for the physical cuts. The best explanation they could offer was that he was suffering some form of mental breakdown because he could not accept the recent death of a favourite aunt. According to their theories his persistent denial might have produced a number of psychological disorders ranging from automatism (involuntary physical actions), obsessive-compulsive disorder (irrational fears or paranoia and possession) and even Gilles de la Tourette's syndrome (which produces physical and verbal tics, along with foul language). But such rational explanations did not satisfy the family, who brought in a Catholic priest in the belief that their son was possessed by a demon. How else could they explain the scratches on his chest which spelt out the words HELL and SPITE, or the fact that he taunted them in Latin – a language he had never studied?

While the boy writhed in his hospital bed the priest began the Roman Ritual of exorcism, but the struggle was cut short when the boy lashed out with a loosened bedspring, causing a deep gash down the priest's right arm that required more than a hundred stitches. Undaunted, another priest took his place and for 24 successive nights the two priests – Father Walter Halloran and Father William Bowdern – prayed at the boy's bedside. On the final night, Robbie opened his eyes and said calmly, 'He's gone.'

The Catholic Church has distanced itself in recent years from the practice of exorcism and no longer endorses it, while a 1972 Church of England report condemned the practice as 'extremely dubious'. In a notorious British murder case in 1974 in which a mentally unstable individual, Michael Taylor, killed his wife after being subjected to an all-night exorcism, his lawyer criticized the group who had agreed to exorcize him by saying that they had fed 'neuroses to a neurotic'.

But despite such criticisms there are those who still believe that good and evil are constantly at war for the possession of our souls. Father Halloran, who took part in the Robbie Mannheim case, recalled a conversation he had with Father Bowdern at the time in which the latter observed, 'They will never say whether it was, or it wasn't [a genuine case], but you and I know it. We were there.'

Exorcism is a controversial practice and has come under criticism from both the Catholic Church and the Church of England in modern times.

THE REAL EXORCIST

During his 16 years on the front line fighting crime in the South Bronx, New York City cop Ralph Sarchie has seen the darkest side of human nature, but he claims that tackling murderers, drug addicts and armed robbers is easy compared to the fiends he faces off duty. When Sarchie hangs up his gun at the end of his shift he arms himself with what he believes to be the only effective defence against the forces of evil – a vial of holy water and a crucifix, for Sarchie is a real-life exorcist – and the Devil had better watch his step when this guy is on his tail.

EXORCISTS AT WORK

His most dramatic 'cases' are now the basis of a bestseller, *Beware of the Night*, which reads like a hardboiled crime novel, but with demons cast in the role of the bad guys. The book has earned him a reputation as a courageous latter-day crusader among America's Christian right who believe the Devil is behind every evil act on earth, but it has brought condemnation from those who fear that in blaming society's ills on a mythical villain we are absolving ourselves of the responsibility for our own actions.

Father James LeBar, one of four exorcists serving the Archdiocese of New York, stated that exorcisms increased from none in 1990 to 'over 300 hundred' by the turn of the millennium. Each year there are said to be between 800 and 1,300 authorized exorcisms around the world.

In an interview for the Christian network Enigma Radio in October 2005 he offered his theory as to why demonic possessions are on the increase. He believes that more people are 'dabbling in the occult' than ever before, which makes them a target for roaming malevolent entities. The only defence, he says, is a strong religious faith and a diet of daily prayer.

POLICEMEN OF THE SPIRITUAL WORLD

Sarchie claims to have assisted at more than 20 exorcisms where he acted as 'the muscle', restraining the possessed person while a Catholic priest performed the rite. But with his mentor Father Martin recently deceased, he is finding it increasingly difficult to persuade a member

Vital weapons against the forces of evil: a vial of holy water and a crucifix.

Demons can possess extreme physical strength and cunning and ending their possessions can be an immense challenge for even the most experienced exorcists.

of the clergy to agree to perform an exorcism. Priests, he reasons, are the 'policemen of the spiritual world' and he points out that even Jesus performed exorcisms. Protestant clergy are no help either as they only offer what they call 'a deliverance' which involves praying to God to intervene in cases of poltergeist infestation or possession. Only Catholic priests are authorized to confront evil in person, so Sarchie now offers to take on the heavies himself. He is deadly serious about his one-man mission and he sincerely believes that his experience in interrogating killers and rapists has prepared him for the 'real struggle' with an adversary who is more sly and seductive than any conman he has ever confronted. Sarchie believes that the aim of the demonic is to create 'self-doubt and emotional turmoil which eats away at their prey's willpower, paving the way for possession'.

1. Obsession
- individual brooding on irrational fears
- indulging in aberrant behaviour
- indulging in a morbid preoccupation
  with violent crime
- dabbling in the occult such
  as experimenting with
  Ouija boards.

2. Oppression
The senses are assaulted with:
- hideous animal shrieks
- loud noises
- other inexplicable phenomena.

3. Physical Possession
- the victim becomes subject to the greater
  will of the demon
- the victim appears normal until the entity
  is challenged to reveal its true nature
  during the exorcism.

PURIFICATION THROUGH FASTING

In preparation for the rite an exorcist must fast for three days to purify himself. Aside from the mental and emotional strain, he invariably has to subdue the possessed person who may have acquired exceptional physical strength.

One rite took two gruelling hours to cast out the 'unclean spirit' and left the muscular cop shaking and exhausted as if he'd been working out. In one attack it had taken five people to hold the victim down. Such experiences haven't dampened Sarchie's enthusiasm for the work.

According to Sarchie, demonic entities 'can level a house in a second. The amount of power even the lowest demon has is stunning', but they are subject to the limitations imposed on them by God, who 'uses them to test us'. Sarchie says that 'direct confrontation is the only way' to deal with the threat.

Ghosts, he says, are the spirits of the deceased while demons were once angelic beings who have lost their supernatural graces, but not their powers. They range from violent brutes which grunt and growl like the beasts of the earth to those which attack using their intellect. It is Sarchie's assertion that a demon can't masquerade as a friendly spirit for long and must eventually reveal its true nature. At this point the victim will be too weak to help themselves so only an exorcist can compel the entity to depart. Sarchie's strategy is to bind it, meaning that he commands it not to interfere in a manner which sounds suspiciously like that practised by medieval magicians. Evidently the line between magic and religious ritual is a very fine one indeed.

He then breaks contact with the subject of the cleansing so as not to be drawn into a dialogue. From this point on he assumes that anything issuing from the mouth of the victim comes from the demon and so ignores any 'pitiful pleas for help'. He also refuses to look into the eyes of the host for fear of being distracted from his task, claiming that the demon will interpret his gaze as a challenge. This may be a good tactic if the attack is genuine, but if the victim is suffering from any form of psychological disorder, ignoring their distress and avoiding eye contact while berating them might be counterproductive.

DEMONS AND STOCKHOLM SYNDROME

Often the host will see the exorcist as a threat rather than as a rescuer – someone who is intending to cause them psychological and physical pain – and will vigorously resist all efforts to drive the demon from their body. Sarchie believes that they suffer from something similar to Stockholm Syndrome, in which kidnap victims identify with their abductors. Of course, if the individual is suffering a psychological rather than a psychic disorder then their resentment and resistance will be more than justified. A typical case will begin with a frantic phone call from a desperate spouse or family member claiming that their beloved husband, wife or child has undergone a drastic personality change. But Sarchie says he can only intervene when invited to do so by the person suffering from the alleged possession and obviously no demon worth the name is going to allow their host to do that, unless they're spoiling for a fight. However, permission isn't required if their home is the scene of what he calls an 'infestation', meaning that the possessed person has become the focus of demonic (i.e., poltergeist) activity and is likely to cause harm to himself or to other members of the family.

THE HALLOWEEN EXORCISM

Of the 20 cases of alleged demonic possession that Sarchie has dealt with, he considers the most harrowing to be the one he faced on Halloween night in 1991. It began when his late partner, Joe Forrester, a polygraph examiner in the legal aid department, received a phone call from a Catholic priest in wealthy Westchester County, north of New York City.

A young suburban housewife and mother, Gabby Villanova, had been pestered by a sorrowful-sounding spirit by the name of Virginia, who claimed to have been murdered on her wedding night and was seeking to be reunited with her family. Her fiancé had been falsely accused of the murder and had taken his own life while awaiting trial. When pressed by Gabby to name the guilty party the grieving spirit is said to have wailed, 'Must not say!'

Having ensured Gabby's attention, 'Virginia' then manifested in broad daylight while Gabby was alone in the basement. The next time it literally took possession of Gabby against her will. At the time Gabby was sharing her home with a middle-aged woman by the name of Ruth and Ruth's 25-year-old son Carl, who had become engaged to Gabby's daughter. Ruth was said to have 'witnessed' telepathic conversations between Gabby and 'Virginia', whose emotional outbursts were becoming more hysterical. Ruth, of course, only heard Gabby's side of the conversation. Nevertheless, she too was taken in by the heartbreaking story and wept at the sad

Exorcists must purify themselves through fasting and mental preparation before attempting to perform the rite.

and sorry tale. In this particular case, Sarchie considered the entity to be far more persuasive and subtle than any professional con artist that he had encountered in his career with the NYPD.

POSSESSION OR SCHIZOPHRENIA?

Sarchie's staunch Catholicism has clearly coloured his perception of definitions of good and evil, but he is adamant that he can differentiate between neurosis and a genuine case of possession.

According to Sarchie, the trouble with diagnosing a genuine case of possession is that demonic behaviour is virtually indistinguishable from many common mental and emotional disorders, so self-appointed exorcists must make their own on-the-spot psychological evaluations, which many are not qualified to do, or they must rely on 'secular psychiatrists' who don't believe in demons or the Devil.

This leaves the burden of proof with the exorcist, and his only criteria for deciding if a case is genuine or not appears to be the subject's aversion to religious artefacts, fits of foul language and an understandable reluctance to be physically restrained and subjected to being sprayed with holy water and hours of intensive prayer. It's a highly subjective diagnosis of behaviour which mental health professionals would say is far more likely to have a psychological rather than a supernatural explanation, specifically a condition known as undifferentiated schizophrenia. The symptoms of this particularly distressing disorder could all too easily be 'mistaken' for those associated with possession by someone with no medical knowledge as it includes periods of lucidity and the ineffective nature of drugs which are normally effective against schizophrenia.

'THE DEVIL WON'T LET YOU GO'

When asked what advice he would give to would-be exorcists, he answers bluntly that his advice is not to do it unless you can see people suffering and still want to help them.

However, if someone is determined to fight the good fight they should pray for guidance to ensure that the impulse comes from God and not from personal ambition. It shouldn't be simply to witness phenomena or 'to see someone's head spin round'.

THE VENNUM CASE

Sometimes, the uninvited spirit may have a benign purpose. In the summer of 1877, Mary Lurancy Vennum, a 13-year-old girl from Watseka, Illinois, suffered a series of convulsions, falling into a trance-like state for hours at a time.

While she was in this state she spoke of seeing angels and a brother and sister who had died some years earlier. Shortly after this, Lurancy was subdued by a succession of dominant personalities who spoke through her, including a crotchety old woman called Katrina Hogan. The family finally resigned themselves to having their daughter committed to an asylum, but then a neighbouring family named Roff intervened. They persuaded Lurancy's parents to consult a doctor from Wisconsin who had treated their own daughter, who had suffered similar 'fits' in which she demonstrated clairvoyant abilities such as being able to read through a blindfold.

When Dr Stevens visited the Vennum house on 1 February 1878, Katrina Hogan was in control. At first she was cold and aloof, gazing abstractedly into space and ordering Stevens to leave her be. But his persistence paid off and he was able to draw out 'Katrina's' personal history. Soon another personality appeared, a young man named Willie Canning whose hold on Lurancy was erratic. With the parents' permission, Stevens tried hypnosis and Lurancy reasserted herself but remained in a trance.

Lurancy announced that she could see other spirits around her, one of whom was Mary Roff. Lurancy did not know Mary Roff, who had died when Lurancy was just a year old. Mrs Roff was present when her 'Mary' came through, speaking through Lurancy, but there is no suggestion that Lurancy was faking to impress or ingratiate herself with the dead girl's mother. The next morning 'Mary' calmly announced her intention to go 'home'. This naturally created some embarrassment for

Mr and Mrs Vennum who were reluctant to have their daughter 'adopted' by a neighbour, but on 11 February, after much soul searching, the Vennums agreed to let their daughter have her way.

When she arrived at the house, she expressed delight at seeing her old piano and appeared to recognize the relatives who greeted her. But even the most cynical witnesses were astonished to hear 'Mary' greet her old Sunday School teacher using her maiden name which Lurancy could not have known. Intrigued, the family subjected 'Mary' to a barrage of probing personal questions relating to seemingly insignificant incidents in her childhood which even the most imaginative impostor could not have faked. She satisfied them on all counts. She even remembered details of a family holiday and could name the spot where her pet dog had died.

Over the following weeks she recognized personal items that she had owned which Mr and Mrs Roff left unobtrusively in the hope of them being identified, but 'Mary' did more than acknowledge them. She would snatch them up in delight and offer some minor detail related to the item that her parents could verify. It was a phenomenon, a rare example of benign possession which was similar in many ways to recorded cases of reincarnation, except that Mary Roff died when Lurancy was a small child.

On her arrival at the Roff house 'Mary' had predicted that she would be using Lurancy for three weeks after which she would return to the spirit world and allow Lurancy to continue with her life. She kept her word. On the morning of 21 May, 'Mary Roff' vacated the body of her host and Lurancy returned to her parents. She later married and lived a normal happy life, but from time to time Mr and Mrs Roff would pay a visit, at which time their daughter would make an appearance to reassure them that all was well. In gratitude for being allowed to say goodbye to her family, the benign spirit even intervened during the birth of Lurancy's first child, putting her into a trance to alleviate the pain of childbirth.

'The next morning "Mary" calmly announced her intention of going "home" . . .'

SOUL MUSIC

On New Year's Day 1970, the musicologist Sir Donald Tovey gave his expert opinion on the authenticity of certain compositions by Beethoven and Liszt which had reputedly been 'channelled' through London medium Mrs Rosemary Brown. The only problem was that Sir Donald Tovey had been dead for some years when he gave this 'lecture'.

By all accounts Brown was a pianist of moderate ability and her knowledge of music was rudimentary at best. Yet for the last five years she had been taking dictation from Liszt, Beethoven, Chopin, Schubert, Brahms and Debussy at a speed she could barely keep up with and, according to a number of influential musicologists, in their distinctive style.

There was one problem, however, and this appears to be the key to the whole mystery. The music was 'first class' according to one critic, but it was not music of genius. If the great composers were active again on the other side, why then did they not produce masterworks rather than highly proficient imitations which any serious music student could conceivably have created?

Although this appears to be a clear case of possession, there is a distinct possibility that it might be an example of split personality disorder. Word association tests carried out by researcher Whately Carington in 1935 with the mediums Osborne Leonard and Eileen Garrett suggest that the 'controls' which mediums claim are the mediators between themselves and the spirits might actually be their own sub-personalities and that these sink back into the unconscious when the dominant personality reclaims control (when the medium wakes from their trance). This would account for the mediums' inability to remember what they had channelled and also for the mysterious appearance of their phenomenal latent talents. At the same time it might also explain why the music was technically impressive, but not works of genius.

Did Sir Donald Tovey give a lecture after his death through the medium Rosemary Brown in 1970?

THE PHANTOM PAINTER

In 1905 Frederick Thompson, an undistinguished amateur English artist, began to paint remarkable pictures in the style of the celebrated Robert Swain Gifford, who had recently died. The two artists had met briefly, but Thompson was not familiar with Gifford's work. It was only when he visited an exhibition of Gifford's work that he saw the similarity between his new creations and that of the dead artist. While studying one of Gifford's pictures Thompson heard a voice in his head urging him to continue his work. 'You see what I have done. Can you not take up and finish my work?'

A painting by Robert Swain Gifford. Frederick Thompson began painting in a similar style after the artist's death, despite never having encountered his work before.

It was the same voice Thompson had been hearing for the past 18 months which had suggested the subjects he was to paint. Thompson feared he was going out of his mind, but the paintings were far more accomplished than he had previously been able to create.

THE ARTIST WITHIN

Automatic art, or automatism to give it its clinical name, is not a recent phenomenon. In the 1930s, the American psychiatrist Dr Anita Muhl experimented with the technique to see if she could connect with her mentally ill patients. Against the expectations of her medical colleagues, many of Dr Muhl's patients produced impressive prose, paintings, sketches and musical compositions with their passive hand (the one they did not normally use to write with), with both hands simultaneously, occasionally writing and drawing upside down or even backwards. A number of patients were even able to draw 'blind', without looking at the paper. All of this was done fluidly, at great speed and without error. Dr Muhl believed that these latent talents originated in the unconscious, but there are those on the fringes of the scientific community who suspect that there might be spirits or a past-life personality at work.

FEATS OF AUTOMATIC ART

- Antiques dealer John Tuckey completed epic Dickensian novels in a distinctive 19th-century copperplate script in a matter of weeks.
- Brazilian automatic artist Luiz Gasparetto can produce two paintings in the style of different great masters simultaneously, one working upright and the other created upside down. Often Gasparetto produces sketches worthy of Cézanne or Manet using only his fingers and toes in less than a minute.

THE THREE CLARAS

When psychiatrist Morton Prince placed patient Clara Fowler under hypnosis, he unwittingly freed two contrasting personalities, each unaware of the other. Clara had been morose, subdued and suffered from depression while her two alter egos could not have been more different. One was considerably more mature and self-assured while the second, which identified herself as 'Sally', was a lively and mischievous little girl who would 'possess' Clara at inconvenient moments. Without warning 'Sally' would take over for hours at a time and when Clara regained control she would find herself in another part of town, bewildered as to how she got there. At the height of her influence, 'Sally' moved to another town, secured a job as a waitress for two weeks and then vacated her host who consequently had to talk her way out of a job she hadn't applied for and find her own way back home.

Spiritualists might interpret these experiences as evidence of possession, while a psychiatrist would regard them as sub-personalities, but if they are merely aspects of our unconscious why then do they create a separate personal history for themselves, speak in another voice and exhibit talents which the dominant personality does not possess? Could it be that they are, in fact, transitory memories and talents from that person's former lives which have been reawakened?

THE QUESTION OF REINCARNATION

In post-war Britain the concept of reincarnation was considered to be an alien idea peculiar to the exotic Eastern philosophies of Hinduism, Shintoism and Buddhism. So when, in 1962, a Catholic father announced that his daughters were living proof of the existence of reincarnation it was seen as a challenge to the authority of the Church which had declared the concept heretical.

John Pollock had lost his first two daughters, Joanna, 11, and Jacqueline, 6, in May 1957 when a driver lost control of her car. A year later, when his wife learnt that she was pregnant, Pollock became convinced that the souls of the two girls would be reborn. When his wife's gynaecologist informed the couple that they were to expect a single child Pollock assured him he was wrong – there would be twins, both girls. On 4 October 1958, he was proved correct.

The twins were monozygotic (meaning they developed from a single egg) yet the second twin, Jennifer, was born with a thin white line on her forehead in the same place that her dead sister Jacqueline had sustained a wound while falling from her bicycle. Her parents were also puzzled by the appearance of a distinctive birth mark on her left hip, identical to the one that Jacqueline had.

The girls grew up in Whitley Bay, but when they were three and a half their father took them back to Hexham and was astonished to hear the girls point out places they had never seen in this life and talk about

When Clara Fowler was put under hypnosis, two very different personalities emerged from her usual subdued self.

where they had played, even though they had left the town before they could walk.

Six months later, they were given Joanna and Jacqueline's toy box. They identified all their dead sisters' dolls by name. They would also play a disturbing game: Jennifer lay on the floor with her head in Gillian's lap, play-acting that she was dying and her sister would say, 'The blood's coming out of your eyes. That's where the car hit you.' Neither parent had discussed the accident with the children. On another occasion their mother saw them clutching each other and looking terrified in the direction of a stationary car with its motor running. The girls were crying, 'The car! It's coming at us!' The incident with the car marked the end of the affair. At the age of five the girls abruptly ceased to seem conscious of the connection with their former lives and developed into normal, healthy children.

This is consistent with a belief that at the age of five all children lose their link with the other world. At this point 'the veil comes down'. Children cease to play with imaginary friends and become grounded in the 'real' world.

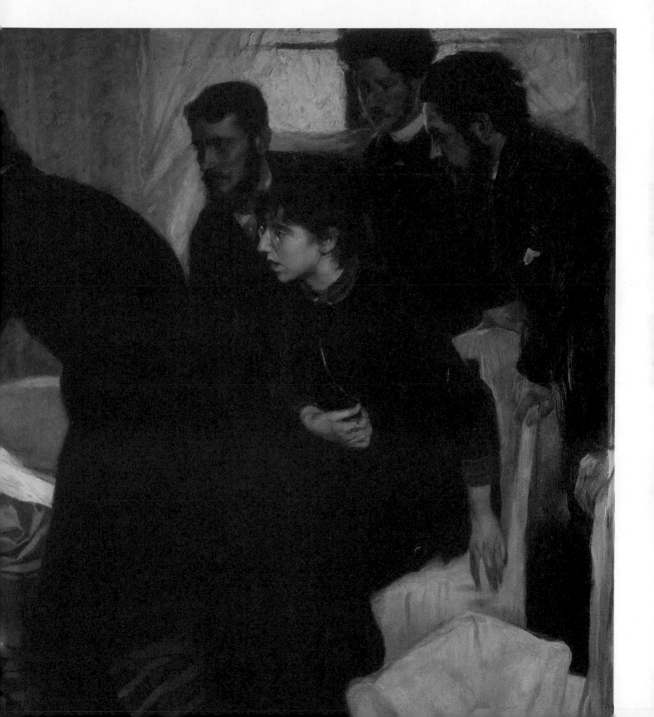

CHAPTER 5

HAUNTED HOUSES

Ghosts do not only haunt crumbling castles,
but have been sighted in the homes of
celebrities, hotels, aircraft, restaurants
and even a Toys "R" Us store.

THE BLOODY TOWER

If any site deserves its formidable reputation for spectral sightings, it is the Tower of London, whose weathered stones are soaked in the blood of countless executed martyrs and traitors. It is said that the walls still echo with the screams of those who were tortured there during the most violent chapters of English history. It is a place of pain where the unquiet souls of those who were imprisoned relive their suffering seemingly for eternity with no prospect of finding peace.

Its long and bloody history began almost 1,000 years ago in 1078 when William the Conqueror built the White Tower in a strategically significant location on the River Thames. Over the next 500 years, the 18-acre site was developed into a formidable fortress within which a succession of kings exercised their divine right over the lives and deaths of their subjects. By the dawn of the 17th century, English royalty had moved to more palatial quarters and the Tower became a soldiers' garrison and prison. On the morning of their execution, condemned prisoners were ceremoniously paraded past jeering crowds to the scaffold erected on nearby Tower Hill where they would be beheaded, or hung, drawn and quartered, and then their bodies would be brought back for burial within the walls of the Tower. These processions of sombre figures have been seen in modern times by sentries who were able to describe accurately the uniforms worn by the burial party.

Among the Tower's most illustrious residents were the

The White Tower was the first structure to be built on the site of the Tower of London and has a long history of hauntings.

Lady Margaret Pole, found guilty of treason, refused to kneel for the executioner and was hacked to pieces in a bloody chase around Tower Green.

young princes Edward and Richard who were declared illegitimate and imprisoned in the so-called Bloody Tower by their ambitious uncle the Duke of Gloucester. Some believe that he ordered their murder so that he could be crowned King Richard III. The princes have been sighted several times walking hand in hand through the chilly corridors after dusk. Given the murdered princes' sense of injustice or revenge, ghosts appear to be an emotional residue rather than a conscious presence.

This is borne out by the nature of the other ghosts which haunt the Tower – they are all victims, not the perpetrators, of the many crimes which took place there. Edward IV, father to the murdered princes, ordered the death of his Lancastrian rival Henry VI on 21 May 1471 at the end of the War of the Roses, but it is not Edward who haunts the oratory in the Wakefield Tower where the killing took place, but Henry who has been seen seated outside the oratory praying that his soul might find peace.

The second wife of Henry VIII is said to still walk in the Tower Chapel where she made her peace with God before she was despatched to his heavenly kingdom in 1536. She is reported to have been seen leading a spectral procession through the chapel both with and without her head.

One of the most gruesome episodes in the Tower's history was the botched execution of Margaret Pole, Countess of Salisbury. Margaret was 70 years old when she was condemned to death in 1541 by Henry VIII, even though she posed no threat to his dynasty. Standing resolutely regal on the scaffold, she refused to submit to the hooded executioner who waited for her to rest her head on the block, but instead she commanded him to sever her head from her neck where she stood. When he refused she fled, forcing him to pursue her around Tower Green swinging the axe like a serial killer in a modern splatter movie. Within minutes the hideous spectacle was at an end; the last female Plantagenet had been hacked to pieces. After dark on 27 May, the anniversary of her execution, the scene is re-enacted by the principal players themselves as Margaret's ghost tries once again to outrun her executioner.

Other apparitions are less active. The headless ghost of James Crofts Scott, the illegitimate son of King Charles II, for example, is said to do little more than walk the battlements connecting the Bell and Beauchamp Towers dressed in cavalier attire. Apparently, James was not satisfied with being made Duke of Monmouth as compensation for losing the crown to his uncle, James II, in 1685, and chose to assert his claim by force of

The princes Edward and Richard, who were imprisoned in the tower and murdered there.

The ghost of Lady Jane Grey has been seen roaming the Tower.

arms. His rebellion was short-lived and he paid for his disloyalty by forfeiting his head.

Arguably the most tragic figure to haunt the site of her untimely death is Lady Jane Grey, who was a pawn in the Duke of Northumberland's stratagem to usurp the English crown from the rightful heir, Mary Tudor. Lady Jane, who was only 15, ruled for less than two weeks before she was arrested and condemned to death together with her young husband and his father in February 1554. Her grieving ghost has been sighted by reliable witnesses on several occasions. In 1957,

two sentries swore they witnessed the apparition of the young queen form from a ball of light on the roof of the Salt Tower while others have reported seeing the spirit of the Duke sobbing at the window of the Beauchamp Tower as he had done on the morning of his execution.

In 1592, Queen Elizabeth I ordered Sir Walter Raleigh to be thrown into the Tower, but upon his release he continued to bait the queen in the belief that he was too popular to be executed. After Elizabeth's death, James I lost patience with Raleigh's preening and boasting and had him convicted on a trumped-up

Sir Walter Raleigh, one of the Tower's many spectral inhabitants.

charge of treason. He was eventually freed in 1616 on condition that he journeyed to the New World in search of gold to fill the royal coffers, but he ignored the king's express orders not to plunder from England's Spanish allies and was beheaded on his return. His ghost still walks the battlements near what were once his apartments in the Bloody Tower.

Not all of the Tower's non-corporeal residents have returned because they cannot rest or because they desire revenge. The ghost of Henry Percy, 9th Earl of Northumberland, has been sighted strolling amiably on the roof of the Martin Tower where he enjoyed walks during his enforced incarceration which began in 1605. Percy, who had been implicated in the Gunpowder Plot, was one of the few prisoners to have been allowed to keep his head and he whiled away the days debating the latest advances in science and other subjects with other educated nobles until his release 16 years later. Percy owed his release to his willingness to pay a fine of £30,000. Since he is clearly reluctant to leave the Tower centuries after his death, perhaps he feels he hasn't had his money's worth.

THE GHOSTS OF GLAMIS

If the typical collection of 'true' ghost stories is to be believed, every castle in the British Isles has its own resident ghost. Whether there is any truth in that or not, Glamis Castle in Scotland certainly has more than its share.

Glamis is the oldest inhabited castle north of the border and is renowned for being both the setting for the tragedy of *Macbeth* and also the ancestral home of the late Queen Mother, Elizabeth Bowes-Lyon. It also has an unenviable reputation as the most haunted castle in the world. Not all the ghosts are tortured souls. In the Queen Mother's sitting room the ghost of a cheeky black servant boy has been sighted playing hide and seek. There is no doubt that the legends of Glamis provide more gruesome thrills than an old-fashioned Gothic thriller. However, fact and fiction are so creatively intertwined that it is now impossible to know which is which.

Several visitors and guests have been distressed by the apparition of a pale and frightened young girl who has been seen pleading in mute terror at a barred window. Legend has it that she was imprisoned after having had her tongue cut out to keep her from betraying a family secret – but what that secret might be remains a mystery. In the 1920s, a workman was said to have accidentally uncovered a hidden tunnel and to have been driven to the edge of insanity by what he found there. Allegedly, the family bought his silence by paying for his passage to another country. There are also tales of a hideously deformed heir who was locked in the attic and an ancient family curse of which the 15th Earl is reputed to have said: 'If you could only guess the nature of the secret, you would go down on your knees and thank God that it was not yours.'

The family's troubles are believed to date from 1537 when the widow of the 6th Lord Glamis was accused of witchcraft and burned at the stake. From that day to this her ghost has been seen on the anniversary of her death on the roof of the clock tower, bathed in a smouldering red glow. Several of the castle's 90 rooms have a dark and bloody history. King Malcolm II of Scotland was murdered in one of them and the floor was boarded because the bloodstains could not be scrubbed clean. It is thought that this may have been the inspiration for the murder of King Duncan, Thane of Glamis, in Shakespeare's play *Macbeth*.

During the years of inter-clan warfare, the castle acquired an entire chamber of vengeful spirits when

men from the Ogilvy clan were given refuge from their enemies in the dungeon, but were then betrayed by their host who walled them up alive. When the wall was torn down a century later, it is said that their skeletons were found in positions which suggested that they had been gnawing on their own flesh. The Scottish novelist

Sir Walter Scott, who considered himself a hardy adventurer, braved a night there in 1793 and lived to regret it: 'I must own, that when I heard door after door shut, after my conductor had retired, I began to consider myself as too far from the living, and somewhat too near the dead.'

THIRTEEN GUESTS

The Winchester Mansion in San Jose, California is unique among haunted houses. It was built by ghosts. Haunted houses are usually host to the restless spirits of their previous occupants, but in the case of the Winchester Mystery House, as it is known locally, its ghosts were not only invited to make themselves at home, they even directed the owner as to how they wanted the house built.

In 1884, Mrs Winchester was grieving for the loss of both her son and her husband who had made his fortune manufacturing the famous Winchester repeating rifle – 'The gun that won the West'. In her grief Mrs Winchester became convinced that the restless spirits of those killed by her husband's weapons would torment her unless she devoted the rest of her life to extending the mansion according to their wishes so that they could while away eternity in comfort.

Every evening she presided over a spooky supper at a long dining table laid for 13, herself and 12 invisible guests. The servants indulged her eccentricities as they were allowed to partake of the leftovers. After dinner the widow conducted a private séance to hear the spirits' latest plans which she would interpret for the workmen the next morning. Either the spirits had a sense of mischievous humour or else Mrs Winchester may have been deliberately trying to disorientate her guests. The house features a number of staircases leading up to the ceiling and doors which open on to a brick wall or a sheer drop. In one particular room there is a single entrance but three exits on the facing wall, one of which leads to an 8 ft (2.4 m) drop into the kitchen on the floor below and another into a windowless room. The door to this room has no handle on the other side, perhaps to entrap a curious ghost or because Mrs Winchester believed it wouldn't need a doorknob as a ghost could supposedly float through the door!

The ghosts seem to have had an obsession with the number 13. They demanded that every new staircase should have 13 steps and new rooms must have 13 win- The chandeliers should boast 13 bulbs and the same number of coat hooks should be available in case they needed to hang up their spectral jackets. There were even 13 fan lights in the greenhouse in case the spirits fancied a spell of hothouse horticulture.

By the time Mrs Winchester passed away on 5 September 1922 at the age of 82, she had devoted the last 38 years of her life to extending the mansion which by then had grown to 160 rooms.

In the 1990s, a pair of paranormal investigators stayed

overnight in the house and were aroused by music from a ghostly organ which, on examination, proved to be disconnected. Moments later they were unnerved by a violent disturbance as the house was shaken to its foundations. In the morning they asked the tour guides if any damage had been caused by the earthquake and were dumbfounded to learn that no tremors had been reported in the area, although in 1906 the destructive San Francisco earthquake had struck at the very same time and severely damaged part of the house.

Not surprisingly, the mansion has become a popular tourist attraction, and the guides are ready to assure visitors that at least three spirits walk the house – a young female servant, a carpenter who died at the site and the indomitable Mrs Winchester, whom staff have seen in Victorian dress, sitting at a table. When they asked their colleagues why they needed someone dressed up as Mrs Winchester they were told that no one was employed to dress up and play the part.

BORLEY RECTORY

During the 1930s and 1940s, Borley Rectory acquired a sinister reputation as 'The Most Haunted House in England'. This unimposing vicarage near Sudbury, Essex, was built in 1863 on the site of a Benedictine monastery which had a dark and unholy history. It was said that a Borley monk had seduced a local nun and the pair had planned to elope. They were caught and the monk was executed and the nun was walled up alive in the cellar.

The first incumbent of the new rectory was the Reverend Bull. He sometimes observed the materializations of the weeping woman as she wandered the gardens searching for her dead lover. Bull often invited guests to join him on his ghost watch. Bull's four daughters and his son Harry resigned themselves to regular sightings of the forlorn spirit drifting across

An affair between monk and nun in the old Benedictine monastery had a tragic ending.

The sinister vicarage of Borley Rectory holds a dark and terrible past.

Ghost hunter extraordinaire: the British psychic investigator Harry Price, who dealt with numerous poltergeist cases during his long and often controversial career looking into the paranormal.

the lawn in broad daylight, but when it was joined by a spectral coach and horses galloping up the drive, the surviving Bull children decided to move on.

At the end of the 1920s, the Reverend Eric Smith and his wife took up residence, shrugging off stories of phantom carriages and sobbing nuns. They had barely had time to unpack their belongings before they ran into a burst of poltergeist activity. However, during their two-year tenure they took the unusual step of calling in the man who was to ensure Borley a place in paranormal history – ghost hunter extraordinaire Harry Price.

Price was a notorious self-publicist and one-time music hall conjurer who hoped to make a name for himself by exposing fake mediums and debunking the spiritualist movement. The more he saw, however, the more convinced he became that some of it was genuine. Eventually, he came to the conclusion that he was more likely to fulfil his ambition of getting into *Debrett's* (a directory of the rich and famous) if he could find proof of life after death.

At the invitation of the Reverend Smith, and later with the encouragement of the next tenants Mr and Mrs Foyster, Price recorded incidents involving phantom footsteps, flying objects and even physical attacks: on one notable occasion Mrs Foyster was even turned out of bed by an invisible assailant. She was also the subject of unintelligible messages scrawled on the walls. Her husband had the house exorcized but the spirits persisted. The servants' bells rang of their own accord and music could be heard coming from the chapel even though no one was in the building. The Foysters admitted defeat and left the spooks in peace. Subsequent owners fared little better. Eventually, the house burned down in a mysterious fire in 1939 as predicted by a spirit 11 months earlier during a séance conducted on the site by Price. Witnesses stated that they saw phantoms moving among the flames and the face of a nun staring from a window.

Borley Rectory ablaze in 1939.

The Daily Mirror

FRIDAY, JUNE 14, 1929

WEIRD NIGHT IN 'HAUNTED' HOUSE

FROM OUR SPECIAL CORRESPONDENT

There can no longer be any doubt that Borley Rectory, near here, is the scene of some remarkable incidents. Last night Mr Harry Price, Director of the National Laboratory For Psychical Research, his secretary Miss Lucy Kaye, the Reverend G.F. Smith, Rector of Borley, Mrs Smith and myself were witnesses to a series of remarkable happenings. All these things occurred without the assistance of a medium or any kind of apparatus. And Mr Price, who is a research expert only and not a spiritualist, expressed himself puzzled and astonished at the results. To give the phenomena a thorough test however, he is arranging for a séance to be held in the rectory with the aid of a prominent London medium.

The first remarkable happening was the dark figure that I saw in the garden. We were standing in the Summer House at dusk watching the lawn when I saw the 'apparition' which so many claim to have seen, but owing to the deep shadows it was impossible for one to discern any definite shape or attire. But something certainly moved along the path on the other side of the lawn and although I quickly ran across to investigate it had vanished when I reached the spot.

Then as we strolled towards the rectory discussing the figure there came a terrific crash and a pane of glass from the roof of a porch hurtled to the ground. We ran inside and upstairs to inspect the room immediately over the porch but found nobody. A few seconds later we were descending the stairs, Miss Kaye leading, and Mr Price behind me when something flew past my head, hit an iron stove in the hall and shattered. With our flash lamps we inspected the broken pieces and found them to be sections of a red vase which, with its companion, had been standing on the mantelpiece of what is known as the Blue Room which we had just searched. Mr Price was the only person behind me and he could not have thrown the vase at such an angle as to pass my head and hit the stove below.

We sat on the stairs in darkness for a few minutes and just as I turned to Mr Price to ask him whether we had waited long enough something hit my hand. This turned out to be a common moth ball and had apparently dropped from the same place as the vase. I laughed at the idea of a spirit throwing moth balls about, but Mr Price said that such methods of attracting attention were not unfamiliar to investigators.

Finally came the most astonishing event of the night. From one o'clock till nearly four this morning all of us, including the rector and his wife, actually questioned the spirit or whoever it was and received at times the most emphatic answers. A cake of soap on the washstand was lifted and thrown heavily onto a china jug standing on the floor with such force that the soap was deeply marked. All of us were at the other side of the room when this happened. Our questions which we asked out loud were answered by raps apparently made on the back of a mirror in the room and it must be remembered though that no medium or spiritualist was present.

Bones were found in the cellar of the rectory and, in an effort to quieten the ghost, given a decent burial in Liston churchyard in 1945, attended by the Rev. A.C. Henning, two local residents and Harry Price.

THE WHITE HOUSE

When the tour guides in Washington DC talk of the White House being haunted by the ghosts of former US presidents they are not speaking metaphorically, neither are they being melodramatic. It is known that Eleanor Roosevelt held séances in the White House during World War II and she claimed to be in contact with the spirit of Abraham Lincoln. During the Roosevelt residency their guest Queen Wilhelmina of the Netherlands was awoken in the night by a knock on her bedroom door. Thinking that it might be Eleanor Roosevelt she got out of bed, put on her nightgown and opened the door. There, framed in the doorway and looking as large as life, was the ghost of Abe Lincoln. Queen Wilhelmina's reaction is not recorded.

Winston Churchill was a frequent visitor to the White House during World War II and he often indulged in a hot bath, together with a cigar and a glass of whisky. One evening he climbed out of the bath and went into the adjoining bedroom to look for a towel when he noticed a man standing by the fireplace. It was Abraham Lincoln. Unperturbed, Churchill apologized for his state of undress: 'Good evening, Mr President. You seem to have me at a disadvantage.' Lincoln is said to have smiled and tactfully withdrew.

The wife of President Calvin Coolidge entertained guests at the White House with her recollections of the day she entered the Oval Office and saw Lincoln looking out across the Potomac with his hands clasped behind his back – a habit he acquired during the Civil War. Lincoln himself was a firm believer in the afterlife and enthusiastically participated in séances during his tenure in office prior to his assassination in 1865. He confided to his wife that he had a premonition of his own death. He dreamt that he was walking through the White House when he heard the sound of weeping coming from the East Room. When he entered he saw

an open coffin surrounded by mourners and guarded by a detachment of Union soldiers. He asked one of the guards who it was who lay in the coffin, to be told, 'The president. He was killed by an assassin.' Lincoln then approached the coffin and saw his own corpse.

President Harry Truman often complained that he was prevented from working by Lincoln's ghost who would repeatedly knock on his door when he was attempting to draft an important speech. Truman wasn't known for his sense of humour and no one would have thought of playing practical jokes during his tenure in the Oval Office so it is assumed he was in earnest.

In the 1960s, Jacqueline Kennedy admitted that she had sensed Lincoln's presence on more than one occasion and 'took great comfort in it'. It is thought that Lincoln's ghost might be drawn to the White House because his son Willie died there and it is reported that the son has himself been seen wandering the corridors in search of his father.

ALCATRAZ

Long before Alcatraz Island in San Francisco Bay was converted into a prison to house America's most notorious criminals, Native Americans warned the US army not to build a fortress on 'the Rock' as it was the dwelling place of evil spirits. Needless to say, their warnings were ignored. When the fortress was converted into a military prison in 1912, several soldiers were said to have been driven insane by mysterious noises in the night, by cold spots which turned their breath to mist even on warm summer evenings and by the sight of two burning red eyes which appeared in the cells on the lower level.

By 1934, the spirits had company when the Rock re-opened for business to house the most notorious gangsters of the Prohibition era including 'Scarface' Al Capone and Machine Gun Kelly. But even the most hardened inmates feared being thrown into 'the hole', the windowless cells of D Block where the red-eyed

demon was said to be waiting to consume lost souls.

On one memorable night during the 1940s a prisoner was hurled screaming into solitary in 14D and continued yelling until early the next morning. When the guards finally opened his cell, they found him dead with distinctive marks around his throat. An autopsy was conducted and the official cause of death was determined to be 'non-self-inflicted strangulation'. When the prisoners were lined up for roll-call the next morning the number didn't tally. There was one extra prisoner in the line. So a guard walked along the line looking at each face to see if one of the inmates was playing a trick on him. He came face to face with the dead man who had been strangled in the night and who promptly vanished before his eyes.

Despite the warden's boast that the prison was escape-proof, several inmates tried to break out and died in the attempt. Their ghosts are said to haunt the hospital block where their bodies were taken. Other

'. . . Native Americans warned the US army not to build a fortress on "the Rock" as it was the dwelling place of evil spirits.'

'Other parts of the prison are host to the unquiet spirits of the five suicides and eight murders which took place before the prison was closed in 1963.'

parts of the prison are host to the unquiet spirits of the five suicides and eight murders which took place before the prison was closed in 1963.

Since the Rock opened to tourists, visitors have claimed to have seen cell doors closing by themselves and to have heard the sound of sobbing, moaning and phantom footsteps, the screams of prisoners being beaten as well as the delirious cries of those made ill or driven insane by their confinement. Others have spoken of seeing phantom soldiers and prisoners pass along the corridors and out through solid walls, and many have complained of being watched even though the corridors and cells were empty.

Those brave enough to try out one of the bunks for size have found themselves pinned down by a weight on their chest as the previous occupant made his presence known. In the lower cells, 12 and 14 in particular, even the least sensitive tourists have admitted to picking up feelings of despair, panic and pain. Whenever a thermometer has been placed in cell 14D it has consistently measured between 20–30 degrees colder than the other cells in that block.

And what of the Rock's most notorious inmate, 'Scarface' Capone? Well, Capone may have been a 'big shot' on the outside but in the 'big house' he was apparently a model prisoner who sat quietly on his bunk in cell B206 learning to play the banjo. It is said that if you sit quietly in that cell you can hear the ghostly strains of Capone whiling away eternity playing popular tunes of the Roaring 20s.

TOYS "R" US

It is a common misconception that ghosts only inhabit crumbling castles and mouldering mansions. The modern Toys "R" Us superstore in Sunnyvale, California occupies a substantial plot on what had been a ranch and an apple orchard back in the 19th century. The poltergeist activity that has been witnessed there is connected with the previous owner John Murphy who, it appears, disliked children, as well as the commercial development of his former home.

Each morning, employees arrive to find stock scattered across the floor and items placed on the wrong shelves. Turnover in staff increased when sensitive workers heard a voice calling their name and were then touched by invisible hands. It was the unwanted attentions of a phantom who assaulted female staff in the ladies' washroom that brought the matter to the attention of the local press and ghost buffs around the globe in 1978.

Local journalist Antoinette May and psychic Sylvia Brown camped out in the store overnight with

'Each morning, employees arrive to find stock scattered across the floor and items placed on the wrong shelves.'

a photographer and a number of ghost catchers. Once the staff had left for the night, Sylvia began to sense a male presence approaching the group. In her mind's eye, she 'saw' a tall, thin man striding down the aisle towards her with his hands in his pockets. In her head she heard him speak with a Swedish accent, identifying himself as Johnny Johnson and warning her that she would get wet if she stayed where she was. It later emerged that a well had existed on that spot. Sylvia established such a strong connection with Johnson that she was able to draw out his life history. He had come to California in the mid-1800s from Pennsylvania, where he had worked as a preacher before succumbing to an inflammation of the brain which affected his behaviour. This appears to account

for his antics in the aisles and the ladies' washroom, as well as the nickname 'Crazy Johnny', given to him by locals at the time.

Johnny lived out his later years working as a ranch hand for John Murphy, pining for a woman named Elizabeth Tafee who broke his heart when she left him to marry a lawyer. Johnny was 80 when he died from loss of blood after an accident with an axe while chopping wood.

Infrared photographs appear to show the figure of a man in the aisles of the store. Surprisingly, the publicity surrounding the haunting hasn't put off the customers, and it has allayed the fears of the employees who are no longer upset by the disturbances – they now know it's only 'Crazy Johnny'.

THE EDGAR ALLAN POE HOUSE

The spirit of Edgar Allan Poe, author of *The Fall of the House of Usher* and other tales of terror, haunts both American fiction and the house in Baltimore where he lived as a young man in the 1830s. The narrow two-and-a-half-storey brick house at 203 North Amity Street is said to be so spooky that even local gangs are scared to break in. When the police arrived to investigate a reported burglary in 1968 they saw a phantom light in the ground floor window floating up to reappear on the second floor and then in the attic, but when they entered

the property there was no one to be seen.

Local residents have also reported seeing a shadowy figure working at a desk at a second-floor window, and the curator has recorded many incidents of poltergeist activity. Doors and windows have opened and closed by themselves, visitors have been tapped on the shoulder and disembodied voices have been heard. Psychic investigators have also reported seeing a stout, grey-haired old woman dressed in clothing of the period gliding through the rooms.

HAUNTED HOMES

If you think that ghosts are only to be found in places that were built a long time ago, think again. Today's spectral squatters are more likely to take up residence in a suburban semi where they can make a real nuisance of themselves. And if it's your home that's haunted, don't blame your uninvited guests – they may just have taken exception to your chosen colour scheme or even your taste in music. So prepare to consult a Ouija board the next time you're considering a makeover.

IN EVERY HOME
A HEARTACHE

The days when ghosts swept through cobwebbed corridors rattling rusty chains are long gone. Today's restless spirits are more likely to karaoke with MTV if they don't get the respect and recognition they believe they deserve. At least that's the message delivered by the late Professor Broersma, who died just before Christmas 1987 in the house he built at 2115 Martingale Drive in a suburb of Oklahoma. A house which he later returned to haunt until the new owners wised up to what he wanted.

The professor found it difficult to communicate at first. There were several new residents of the house in quick succession, each driven out by inexplicable noises and occurrences until, in 1994, newly-weds Jon and Agi Lurtz moved in. Jon and Agi were not put off by tales of a restless spirit or the fact that one previous owner had reportedly fled leaving all his earthly possessions behind.

The professor's campaign of intimidation began with regular radio broadcasts in the middle of the night – and it was loud, very loud. Try as they might, the couple couldn't locate the source of the signal. Their own radio was unplugged. What's more, it was not a station they recognized. It was broadcasting old news from years gone by.

Having failed to dislodge the couple, the ghost tried a new tactic. He took possession of the hi-fi and began blasting out heavy metal music at ear-bleeding volumes. His favourite band apparently was the German technogrunge group Rammstein, whose aural assault of overdriven guitars threatened to bring down plaster from the ceiling. Jon and Agi would frequently return from a shopping trip to find the hi-fi going at full blast, but the equipment had always been switched off before they had left.

One night in 1998 Agi awoke to see the figure of a man standing at the foot of her bed and, assuming it to be the professor, she demanded to know what he wanted. In a foreign accent he replied that all he wanted was an obituary as he had never had one. And with that he faded away.

Later that day Agi began to research the professor's past. She discovered that his death had not been reported in the local paper and no acknowledgement of his considerable achievements had been made. During World War II the Dutch-born academic had served with distinction in the resistance movement after which he moved to America. There he contributed to the development of advanced sensor technology for NASA (National Aeronautics and Space Administration).

All of these accomplishments were listed in Agi's glowing obituary which she wrote for the local paper. They were also included in the eulogy she read aloud at a belated memorial service that she arranged to commemorate his life. It was all the brooding spirit wanted, for immediately afterwards the disturbances ceased.

Some people prefer to keep their achievements to themselves, but clearly the professor felt that he was overdue some recognition before he could rest in peace.

HOUSE BY THE CEMETERY

Ben and Jean Williams moved into their dream home in 1983. The new development at Newport, Texas was within commuting distance of Houston and boasted immaculate landscaped gardens and highly desirable upmarket homes. But there was a catch. Their garden seemed to attract an unusual number of poisonous snakes. Lights would switch themselves on and off, the garage door repeatedly malfunctioned and the atmosphere felt unusually oppressive. They could not shake off a sense of foreboding or the feeling that something, or someone, was watching them.

Whenever something inexplicable occurred, they came up with a rational explanation. The lights and garage door could be due to faulty wiring, the snakes to some natural phenomenon and their paranoia to the stress of moving.

But there was no explanation for the series of large rectangular holes which seemed to form a pattern in their lawn. As soon as they filled them in, the soil would drain out of them, leaving the same grave-shaped impressions. Their unspoken suspicions finally surfaced when contractors began excavating the backyard of the home belonging to their neighbours Sam and Judith Haney and unearthed a pair of rotting coffins containing the corpses of a man and a woman.

The following day, their curiosity aroused, the Newport neighbours banded together to make inquiries into the history of the site and discovered that it had once been the last resting place of poor black citizens of that region, many of them former slaves.

They even managed to locate a retired black gravedigger who was able to identify the disinterred remains as those of Bettie and Charlie Thomas, who had died during the Depression. Out of genuine respect for the deceased, the Haneys insisted that the bodies be reburied in the garden and given a decent Christian funeral service. But that did not appear to have appeased the dead couple, or to pacify the 60 or so former occupants of Newport's Black Hope Cemetery. Over the following days the Haneys were subjected to a barrage of poltergeist activity: a clock spat sparks, phantom footsteps marched up and down the empty rooms after dark and a pair of Judith's shoes disappeared only to turn up on Bettie's freshly dug grave. That was it for the Haneys. They instigated legal action against the developer and won the case,

but it was overturned on appeal, so they packed up and moved out, leaving a perfectly good house to the ghosts.

Meanwhile, Ben and Jean Williams were seriously considering selling up and moving out, but rumours of the weird goings-on had spread through the real estate community and no one was interested in having the

A series of unmarked graves were found in the garden of the Williamses' house.

house on their books. Then one night Ben returned home late to see a figure standing at the end of his bed while his wife slept. It was the last straw. They decided that if they were to succeed where their neighbours had failed in suing the developer they would have to provide physical proof. So, in the belief that other bodies were buried in their back garden, they decided to unearth these themselves. Jean began digging one afternoon but found the task too tiring so she gave the spade to her 30-year-old daughter, Tina. After only a short while Tina complained of breathlessness and chest pains, then collapsed. She died two days later. The Williams family moved out shortly afterwards and settled in Montana.

PHANTOM PHOTOS

Little Lisa Swift hated piano lessons. It wasn't the practice – it was the accompanist she objected to, a 7,000-year-old Native American who played a discordant and haunting tune on his wooden flute whenever she sat down to play. Shadows seemed to follow her from room to room accompanied by the sweet scent of burning wood. But none of these unsettling scents or sounds bothered her mother, Rita, until much later. In the summer of 1969 Rita was too preoccupied with her new hobby, taking photographs of the family home and the pet cat. She used an old Kodak Brownie Hawkeye and the film was standard black and white stock. So maybe it was something in the quality of the light in the backyard that September, or maybe there was a fault in the film or the camera because there was no rational explanation for the images which appeared on the last three frames when the negative was developed 30 years later.

Of course, it might have been the delay in processing the film which created the ghostly apparitions. Fogging is a common fault in amateur photography caused by light leaking into the camera casing and these milky white streaks have been mistaken for ghosts in the past. But the prints Rita Swift collected from the photo shop in 1999 were pin sharp and the strangers she had unknowingly photographed all those years ago were certainly not her neighbours.

The first shot showed three Native Americans in traditional costume dancing in a line. The other two captured a tribe in ceremonial dress grouped around a row of bodies prepared for ritual cremation. The thought occurred to Rita that someone at the photo store must have been playing a prank, but the other images on the roll were all of her own family. It couldn't have been tampered with by anyone in the family as she had locked the camera with the film still inside it in a trunk in September 1969 and no one had touched it until she found it by accident 30 years later.

When she plucked up the courage to show the photos to Native Americans living nearby they refused to look at them more closely, for fear of intruding on a sacred ceremony. If the Swift home had been built on a Native American burial ground it would explain the ghostly flute and the smell of burning wood. Charred bones were unearthed in the Swifts' backyard in 1962, five years before the spooky photos were taken. Experts at California State College at Long Beach identified them as the partially cremated remains of a Native American female dating back approximately 7,000 years.

If the Swift home had been built on a Native American burial ground it would explain many things.

CANDID CAMERA

Of course, it would be more convincing if such images were caught on video and that is exactly what occurred early on an October morning in 1991 in a nightclub in Lancashire, northern England. At 4.32 am the burglar alarm at the club was triggered by the appearance of a phantom figure which was evidently sufficiently solid to be picked up by its sensors. When the manager arrived he ordered the night staff to search the building, but no signs of a break-in were found and all the employees could account for their whereabouts at the time. Baffled as to what might have activated the alarm, the manager ordered the surveillance tapes to be played. There for all to see was a ghostly figure moving soundlessly through the corridor and then passing through a solid locked door to the cash office. No explanation has been offered to explain the phenomenon.

THE FACE
IN THE WINDOW

On the morning of 29 April 1997 *Indianapolis Star* photographer Mike Fender had been assigned to record the removal of a historic 19th-century, Gothic Revival-style farmhouse from a hilltop just outside town to a choice location where it could be preserved by the Historic Landmarks Foundation. It was a delicate operation for the hauliers who had to manhandle the fragile 24-room home without dismantling it. Being a methodical and conscientious employee, Fender took several shots from every conceivable angle. Then, as he stood in front of the trailer on which the house had been secured for its short journey, he noticed what he thought was a little girl in a blue dress standing at an upstairs window looking apprehensively at the scene below. But the house was empty.

The next day the story appeared alongside the photo. Fender had had a deadline to meet and he had taken the chance that no one would notice the tiny figure in the window. But he was wrong.

'We got hundreds of calls,' he was later to say. 'Things like this usually fade after a day or two, but this went on and on and on.'

Everyone, it seemed, had a theory. It was the restless spirit of a little girl who had fallen to her death from the balcony; she had been a murder victim or she had been awoken from her eternal rest by the disturbance to her former home. But research by the Historic Landmarks Foundation had failed to unearth any records that would support any of these theories and the numerous inquiries which followed.

Fender subjected the picture to digital analysis. To his puzzlement, after enlarging the image it clearly showed a little girl in a blue dress. Only there was one element of the picture that no one had noticed – the little girl had no face.

The head of the girl appeared to be above the railings, while her body seemed to be behind them.

THE FACE IN THE FLAMES

One of the most startling and controversial phantoms on film was captured by an English amateur photographer, Tony O'Rahilly, during a blaze at Wem Town Hall, Shropshire in November 1995. When he developed the film, there was no mistaking the image of a young girl standing in an open doorway on the fire escape. Two professional photographers (Tony Adams of the *Shropshire Star* and an expert from the *Daily Express*) examined both the print and the negative after which they declared themselves satisfied that it was not a hoax.

Former president of the Royal Photographic Society, Dr Vernon Harrison, then a member of the Association for the Scientific Study of Anomalous Phenomena (ASSAP), stated that he was confident the photograph was genuine. However, Dr Harrison was puzzled by the fact that the head of the girl appeared to be above the railings of the fire escape while her body seemed to be behind them. Also a belt around

her waist looked as if it extended in a line across and beyond her body instead of being wrapped around her. The image hadn't been faked, Dr Harrison concluded, but it was possible that the image was an illusion created by falling debris and tricks of the light. Subsequent examination of the fire service video of the blaze revealed a blackened roof beam where the girl's 'belt' had been, but it did not account for the unmistakable image of her 'face'.

The BBC (British Broadcasting Corporation) was next in line to examine the photo and submitted it to the National Photographic Museum. They pointed out several horizontal lines across the girl's face, which they concluded indicated that it had been computer generated.

Looking closely at the photograph, it is hard to imagine that the image could have been created by smoke and falling debris snapped at just the right moment when it happened to form a clearly discernible face.

CHAPTER 6

SPOOKY SITES

Unquiet spirits rarely linger in graveyards as they do not wish to be reminded of how they died. Some may even be unaware that they are dead. There are certain places in the world that appear to attract a disproportionate number of visitors from the other side.

CITY OF THE DEAD

Every city in the world has its share of ghosts, but surely none is more deserving of its reputation as the capital of the uncanny than Edinburgh. With its narrow, twisting alleyways, cobbled streets and ancient, imposing buildings, the Old Town resembles the set of a Hammer horror movie. All it needs is a shroud of creeping fog and one can imagine its more unsavoury inhabitants stalking the streets again.

Other cities have their serial killers and criminals, but Edinburgh can boast a whole rogues' gallery, enough to fill the chamber of horrors in Madame Tussauds several times over.

Long before Hannibal Lecter put cannibalistic killers on the menu Edinburgh was home to real-life people-eater Sawney Bean. Then there were the bodysnatchers, Burke and Hare, cross-eyed lady killer Dr Thomas Neill Cream and criminal mastermind Deacon Brodie, the inspiration for Robert Louis Stevenson's *Dr Jekyll and Mr Hyde*. In fact several of Edinburgh's larger-than-life personalities served as the models for immortal literary figures, including Sherlock Holmes and his nemesis Professor Moriarty. Conan Doyle studied medicine at Edinburgh University and based the master detective on his own teacher and mentor Dr Joseph Bell. Charles Dickens made only a brief sojourn to the city, but he returned with the seed for what is arguably the most famous ghost story ever written, *A Christmas Carol*. And let's not forget that his spiritual descendant, J.K. Rowling, conjured up her finest creation, the boy wizard Harry Potter, in a café overlooking Greyfriars Graveyard.

But if it's 'real' history you're wanting, then your first stop must be the oldest haunted site in Edinburgh which lies just outside the city. As everyone who has read *The Da Vinci Code*, or seen the movie based on Dan Brown's bestseller, will know, the 15th-century chapel at Roslin is the centre of an alleged conspiracy concerning the true fate of Jesus of Nazareth and his supposed descendants, proof of which is said to be hidden in sealed vaults underneath the chapel. The hype surrounding the book has attracted thousands of tourists from around the world who might not have been so keen to linger had they known that the chapel is haunted by an order of Augustine monks known as the Black Canons. Judith Fiskin, a former archivist and curator at Roslin, claims to have seen a ghostly monk during her tenure in the 1980s and to have shared the experience with several reliable witnesses. But the

The chapel at Roslin is central to the plot of *The Da Vinci Code*.

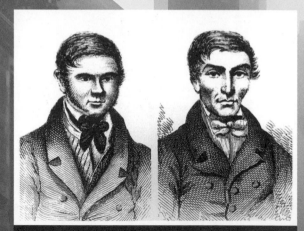

William Burke and William Hare – two of Edinburgh's most notorious serial killers.

brothers are not the only spirits wandering around. The site is also said to be haunted by the restless spirit of a mason's apprentice, reputedly killed by his master for having outshone his mentor by carving what is known as the Apprentice Pillar.

Animal spirits are also to be seen when conditions are favourable. According to local legend the spirit of a murdered hound can be seen and heard prowling the grounds of nearby Roslin Castle. The Mauthe Dog, as

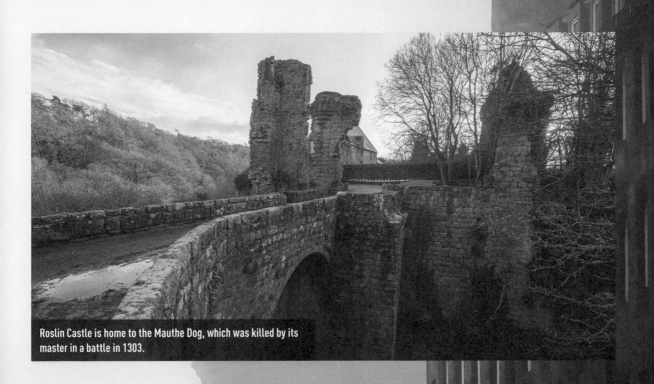

Roslin Castle is home to the Mauthe Dog, which was killed by its master in a battle in 1303.

it is known, was cruelly put to death beside its English master during the Battle of Roslin in 1303 at which the Scots routed an English army of more than 30,000. Bad losers, the Sassenachs.

There is even a local 'white lady' identified as Lady Bothwell who was evicted from her ancestral home by the heartless Regent Moray in the late 16th century. Presumably, she returns to search in vain for her tormentor and tear his merciless heart from his body.

EDINBURGH

+ ☠ +

CITY OF THE DEAD

① BARONY STREET

A local coven known as the 'Witches Howff' were burned alive in a house in this street in the 17th century, just 13 of an estimated 300 women burned for practising the 'old religion' in Edinburgh at the time.

② EDINBURGH CASTLE

The sound of phantom drums and bagpipes besets visitors to the castle as its many sieges are relived again and again. Other apparitions include John Graham of Claverhouse, known as 'Bloody Clavers', and Janet Douglas, Lady Glamis, who was burned at the stake for witchcraft in 1537.

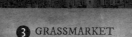

③ GRASSMARKET

The Grassmarket was the site of the execution of the Covenanters as well as a key stalking ground for the serial killers William Burke and William Hare. A phantom coach can be seen passing through as well as the ghost of a woman with a burned face.

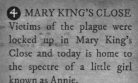

④ MARY KING'S CLOSE

Victims of the plague were locked up in Mary King's Close and today is home to the spectre of a little girl known as Annie.

⑤ GILLESPIE CRESCENT, BRUNTSFIELD

On this site once stood a celebrated haunted house known as The Wrychtishousis. In the 18th century it was the scene for regular visits by a headless woman who was believed to be the wife of James Clerk, who died leaving her and her baby to the tender mercies of his homicidal brother. With James out of the way, the brother murdered her in order to inherit the house, but he brought too short a trunk and had to cut her head off to get her body inside it. Then he hid the box in the cellar. Just another gruesome old legend? Nope. Her headless corpse and that of her child were unearthed by workmen when the house was being demolished, together with the killer's written confession.

EDINBURGH OLD TOWN

FOUNTAINBRIDGE

⑥ ROYAL LYCEUM THEATRE, LOTHIAN ROAD

The actress Ellen Terry is said to haunt the stage on which she made her theatrical debut in 1856.

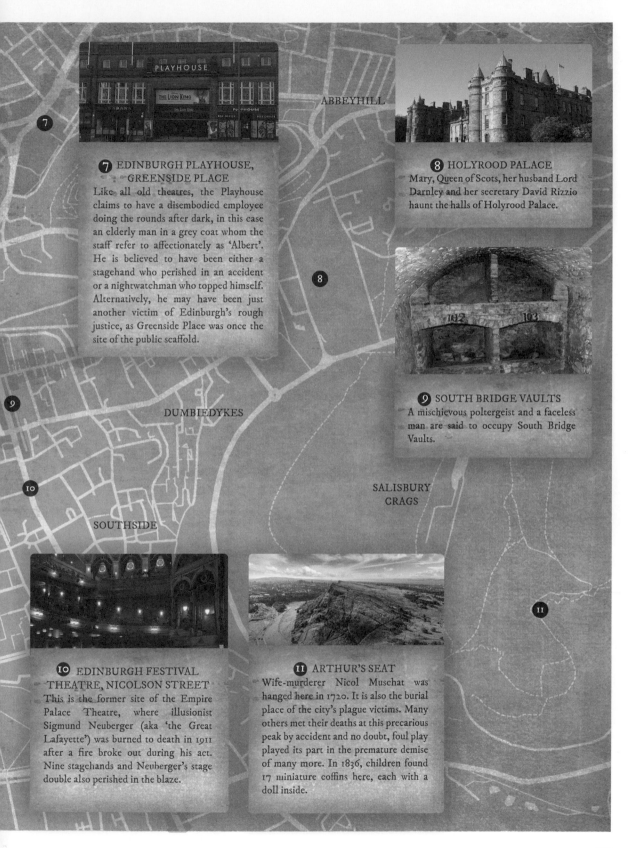

ABBEYHILL

7 EDINBURGH PLAYHOUSE, GREENSIDE PLACE

Like all old theatres, the Playhouse claims to have a disembodied employee doing the rounds after dark, in this case an elderly man in a grey coat whom the staff refer to affectionately as 'Albert'. He is believed to have been either a stagehand who perished in an accident or a nightwatchman who topped himself. Alternatively, he may have been just another victim of Edinburgh's rough justice, as Greenside Place was once the site of the public scaffold.

8 HOLYROOD PALACE

Mary, Queen of Scots, her husband Lord Darnley and her secretary David Rizzio haunt the halls of Holyrood Palace.

9 SOUTH BRIDGE VAULTS

A mischievous poltergeist and a faceless man are said to occupy South Bridge Vaults.

DUMBIEDYKES

SALISBURY CRAGS

SOUTHSIDE

10 EDINBURGH FESTIVAL THEATRE, NICOLSON STREET

This is the former site of the Empire Palace Theatre, where illusionist Sigmund Neuberger (aka 'the Great Lafayette') was burned to death in 1911 after a fire broke out during his act. Nine stagehands and Neuberger's stage double also perished in the blaze.

11 ARTHUR'S SEAT

Wife-murderer Nicol Muschat was hanged here in 1720. It is also the burial place of the city's plague victims. Many others met their deaths at this precarious peak by accident and no doubt, foul play played its part in the premature demise of many more. In 1836, children found 17 miniature coffins here, each with a doll inside.

THE UNDERGROUND CITY

The focus of many of the city's supernatural encounters is the area around Edinburgh Castle known as the underground city. It's a labyrinth of tunnels and cavernous chambers carved out of the crag and tail on which the castle and Royal Mile were built. When overcrowding in the city was at its height in the early years of the 18th century, the poor carved out their own living quarters from the rock. Many perished in the intolerable conditions from hunger, cold, disease and periodic cave-ins. Their spirits are thought to account for the moaning and wailing heard by the shopkeepers brave enough to venture down into their basement stock rooms after dark.

HAUNTED HOT SPOTS

Arguably the most notorious haunted spot in the city is Mary King's Close. The legends associated with this location centre on the victims of the plague of 1645 who were imprisoned by the city elders. Their jailers then locked the gates at both ends of the close for fear that the contagion might spread. None survived. Their

decomposing corpses were later hacked up and buried in an area known as The Meadows.

In 1992 a documentary film crew arrived with a Japanese psychic named Aiko Gibo. In one of the houses, she claimed to see an apparition of a 10-year-old girl wearing a dirty white dress and boots, called 'Annie'. Gibo and Annie communicated telepathically and returned with a new doll, which seemed to comfort the spirit. A short while later a visitor to the site who had known nothing of the broadcast screamed when she entered the room, claiming to have seen a little girl in the corner whose face was disfigured by sores. Research has unearthed the fact that a woman by the name of Jean Mackenzie and her little girl were forcibly quarantined in the house during the plague.

Other shadowy residents of the close include 'The Worried Man', who walks back and forth as if brooding on some dark deed he is planning, or perhaps he is simply searching for something. At other times a woman in black appears for a moment at the end of the close and then just as mysteriously vanishes, as does a young boy at the same location. A male figure, presumably a storekeeper, has been seen suspended in mid-air beneath the 'plague room' window and a middle-aged woman has been known to appear at the top of the steps leading into the street. If anyone is brave enough to venture inside the derelict houses they are sure to hear sufficient scratching, whispering and boisterous phantom carousing to convince them that their former residents are extremely reluctant to leave.

THE HAUNTED VAULT

Marion Duffy and her 6-year-old daughter Claire joined a guided tour to South Bridge Vaults. Despite Marion's doubts, the little girl remained eager to explore even when the party entered the claustrophobic chamber deep underground. She reassured her daughter in the dark and a small hand responded with a gentle squeeze. Then the grip became tighter and tighter until Marion realized that she couldn't pull herself free. It was becoming painful. Instinctively she pulled hard and kicked, not caring in that moment if Claire was hurt as the pain was unbearable. But no child would be capable of such a vice-like grip. She kicked harder and in doing so lost her balance. She collided with the person standing next to her in the dark who screamed that something was attacking her and the next instant there was a mad scramble for the exit.

When the guide switched the torch back on Marion

found herself surrounded by strangers, all with a look of embarrassment on their faces. Claire was nowhere to be seen. Then her mother spotted her on the other side of the vault. Shaking with a mixture of fear and relief, the little girl explained that when the light went out a hand had gripped hers and led her to the far end of the vault. She knew it wasn't her mother's hand, but she had been too frightened to cry out. Asked how she knew it wasn't her mother's hand, she replied, 'Because it had claws.'

Visitors to South Bridge Vaults have reported encountering physical abuse from its resident spirits.

Mary King's Close: shadowy residents include 'The Worried Man' and a lady who appears at the end of the close and then vanishes.

GREYFRIARS GRAVEYARD

Greyfriars is known locally as a 'thin place', a site where the veil between this world and the next is believed to be so fragile that spirits can pass through it. Its reputation presumably grew from the fact that it was the site of mass graves following the great plague of 1568 when countless thousands of diseased corpses were flung into a huge pit.

Twelve hundred survivors of the Covenanter movement (Scots Presbyterians) were imprisoned in the Covenanters' Prison on the orders of Charles II after their defeat at the Battle of Bothwell Brig. Many of them starved to death or died from disease. Of the remainder many thousands were executed by the King's Advocate, 'Bloody' George Mackenzie. Mackenzie was buried in Greyfriars in 1691 within sight of the Covenanters'

Prison and the graves of those he had condemned to death. Not surprisingly perhaps, this inspired a host of macabre ghost stories including one in which 'Bloody' Mackenzie's coffin is said to move within the tomb, known as the Black Mausoleum, because he is restless and tormented in death.

Other visitors complained of feeling gripped around the ankles by an ice-cold band as if they were experiencing what it had felt like to be shackled to the wall in the Covenanters' Prison. Dozens reported that their cameras malfunctioned in certain sites but not in others, while those who managed to capture images of floating balls of light and luminous shapes sent copies to the tour agency and to magazines to prove their claims.

Twelve hundred survivors of the Covenanter movement were imprisoned in the Covenanters' Prison. . . many of them never emerged again.

The Black Mausoleum hides its dark character during daylight.

EYEWITNESS ACCOUNTS

'We had not been in the Black Mausoleum long when we started hearing knocking noises coming from beneath us, which steadily grew louder and seemed to move up and round the walls. I was standing at the back and I felt the temperature drop, even though it was a very warm night. I started physically shaking, even though I was wearing several jumpers, and had pins and needles in my feet and arms. I then felt myself go freezing cold and the next thing I remember is waking up lying on the ground. My friend had also collapsed. The next morning, I woke up to find that I had three deep scratches on my stomach – there is no way this could have been caused by my falling, as I was wearing several layers. My friend Lewis also had scratches on his arm.

I decided to go back again, this time with a group of different friends. I experienced the same sensations – the feeling of cold, pins and needles, and shaking, followed by the inevitable black-out and scratches on my arms the next morning.'

Camilla Davidson

'I still felt quite happy when we entered the Covenanters' Prison. It wasn't until I got into the Black Mausoleum itself that I began to feel uneasy. I felt that someone or something was looking right at me. As I turned to look I saw what can only be described as a hooded figure with a featureless face and a couple of inches shorter than me.'

B Johnson, Coventry

UNINVITED GUESTS

There was once a time when any self-respecting ghost would haunt only the grandest of stately homes. But times change, and today even ghosts must settle for what they can get. Lincoln city council has been inundated with requests from tenants demanding to be relocated to escape spectral squatters who have made their lives a living hell.

Jade Callaby, a 26-year-old single mum, suffered six years of unexplained paranormal activity in her Prial Avenue property. It began with kettles, TVs and toasters switching on by themselves and with objects disappearing from one room only to turn up in another. But then the curious incidents became less playful and more disturbing. Jade and her 9-year-old daughter, Courtney, were startled out of their sleep night after night by loud banging noises. They also claim to have seen shadows when no one else was present in the house.

In desperation Jade called in a priest to 'bless' the house, but the unsettling incidents continued. She was forced to ask the council to relocate her.

'It's been absolutely terrifying. Kettles and vacuum cleaners have turned on and off by themselves, cups have moved, dark shadows have appeared and darkened rooms, and my daughter has been woken up by the sound of heavy breathing in front of her face – but nobody was there. I used to try to explain things away, but now I believe – and I'm not staying there another night.'

– Jade Callaby

THE FORMER TENANT

In March 2000, in a flat in Woolwich, south London, a young mother with a baby daughter complained of being tormented by noises, shadows and inexplicable activity. The hauntings had begun with seemingly insignificant signs, such as her daughter appearing to react to an unseen presence, and the cat running away. She heard footsteps in an empty room above and a shuffling sound outside her bedroom door, and one night the duvet was pulled off. The woman also sensed that someone was watching her from the bottom of the stairs.

One evening, in her bedroom she saw the shadow of a man in the corner. This shadowy presence had substance. He was a black man, wearing a suit, between 30 and 40 years of age, and he appeared to be asleep. He only disappeared after she repeatedly looked away. Another night she woke to see a man standing in the corner of the room, before fading away.

At this point she became convinced that the house was haunted. The previous tenant admitted experiencing a constant feeling of being watched. She said she had found her small son talking to an invisible presence he called Peter; his toy car would shoot across the room on its own and the dog would growl unaccountably at the bottom of the stairs.

A paranormal investigation group, the Ghost Club, asked a psychic to check out the house. As soon as he entered, he felt he was being watched. He traced the presence to the right-hand corner of the bedroom, where the shadow of the man had been seen. He then entered the child's room and felt that the presence had a connection with the child. On 6 July, members of the Ghost Club returned with a number of psychics. They sensed that two previous female tenants had suffered miscarriages; this was subsequently confirmed. In the child's room, they picked up on the presence of a man in black, a sense of panic and someone screaming for help. At 11 pm that night, all the visitors heard footsteps running down the hallway. One had the strong sense that a man had carried on abusive relationships with the women, one of whom had murdered him. According to one of the psychics, his ghostly presence in the bedroom was because he had lived next door and entered the flat from a balcony that led to the bedroom window.

A young mother in London would see a shadowy figure of a man hiding in her bedroom who would appear suddenly and then disappear.

THE MANY GHOSTS OF THE MYRTLES MANSION

The old plantation mansions of the Deep South, particularly those in Louisiana, have a singular atmosphere, shrouded as they are in Spanish moss and veiled in creeping fog seeping in from the bayou. The Myrtles mansion (built in 1796) is perhaps the most haunted in the United States.

Several guests have spoken of being approached by slaves and domestic servants who ask what they can do for the guests, before fading in front of their eyes. A gateman quit the guesthouse after welcoming a lady in a white dress, who walked up to the house and promptly disappeared through the (closed) front door! In the evening the piano has been heard to play one melancholy chord over and over again, but no one is seen sitting at the keyboard.

CHLOE THE SLAVE

In the 1950s the house was sold to a widow, Marjorie Munson, and that is when the ghost stories began. Marjorie was tormented by unexplained occurrences and asked her neighbours if any of them had heard if the house was haunted. There was a local legend of an old woman in a green bonnet, but she had no name; it was only when James and Frances Kermeen purchased the house in the 1970s that the legend of Chloe the slave was born. It was said that Chloe wore the green headband to cover a gaping wound where her ear had been cut off as punishment for eavesdropping. Even more lurid and fanciful was the tale of how the slave had been abused by her master and then abandoned. She was said to have sought revenge by poisoning his three children, a crime for which she was hanged by her fellow slaves. In fact, two of the children she was accused of killing died several years apart and the third

Myrtles mansion in Louisiana is home to a vast array of spirits and lays claim to being the most haunted house in all of the United States.

was not even born at the time of the alleged crime. Exhaustive research by historian David Wiseheart failed to find any record of a slave by the name of Chloe.

BLOOD ON THE FLOORBOARDS

Of the supposed six murder victims named in previous histories of the house, one was found to have died of yellow fever (not stabbed to death over a gambling debt, as local legend would have it); the tale of three Union soldiers who were shot during a looting spree was also exposed as a complete fallacy. In echoes of numerous other ghost stories, it was said that their bloodstains on the floorboards could not be scrubbed clean, but no account of their murder could be found in the local newspapers or military archives. The story of the fifth 'victim', a caretaker killed during an attempted burglary in 1927, may have been inspired

by the murder of a local man in another building on the plantation around the same time.

THE HAUNTED MIRROR

Even though many of the ghosts have been dispatched by diligent research, some enthusiasts remain stubbornly devoted to the mansion's reputation and point to the 'haunted mirror' as evidence of its supernatural cachet. Photographs of this antique-looking mirror appear to show a cluster of phantom hands imprinted behind the glass. When this was pointed out to the present owners, they had the glass professionally cleaned, but the prints could not be erased. They replaced the glass and still the prints were seen when the guests had their snapshots developed. The latest theory is that the impressions are flaws in the wood which appear in the shape of handprints when the flashlight catches the indentations.

The mansion is home to a haunted mirror which shows the impression of phantom hands behind the glass.

THE SILVER QUEEN HOTEL
VIRGINIA CITY, NEVADA

Janice Oberding awoke in the early hours to a couple arguing next door. Janice could hear the man's voice through the wall as well as the woman begging him for forgiveness. After breakfast Janice reported the row to the manager, only to be told that the room next to hers was unoccupied and that the disturbance had been caused by the resident ghosts. Years earlier, a man had murdered his girlfriend in that room.

BALSAMS HOTEL
DIXVILLE NOTCH, NEW HAMPSHIRE

At the Balsams Hotel a female resident woke one morning to see a dripping wet, naked man standing at the foot of her bed. She assumed it was her husband emerging from the shower, but her husband was sleeping next to her. He woke just in time to corroborate her story. The next instant, the naked figure vanished.

THE COPPER QUEEN HOTEL
BISBEE, ARIZONA

Hotels are required to keep a register of their guests, but one hotel in Bisbee, Arizona, keeps a register of its ghosts too. The entries in the ghost register describe many seemingly insignificant but unsettling incidents, such as a child's soft toy playing hide and seek with its owner, and the inexplicable failure of cameras and mobile phones in certain 'dead spots'. There have been various sightings of a ghostly boy called Billy who has been seen jumping on a leather couch in the lobby, decades after he was found drowned in a nearby river. Some guests have reported encountering a bearded man in a top hat, who leaves behind a trail of cigar smoke; other male guests claim to have been 'interfered with' by the ghost of a prostitute who is said to have committed suicide in the hotel. All told, there are said to be 16 spirits haunting Bisbee.

THE RENAISSANCE VINOY
ST PETERSBURG, FLORIDA

Several baseball players encountered unsettling spirits at the palatial, palm-lined Renaissance Vinoy Hotel. Scott Williamson saw a faint luminous glow near the pool through his curtains, and felt as if someone was pushing down on him when he lay down to sleep. He opened his eyes to see a shadowy man standing by the window, dressed in a long coat that seemed to belong to the 1930s or 1940s. Pitcher Frank Velasquez of the Pittsburgh Pirates awoke to see a transparent figure standing by the desk at the window. The team's assistant saw a man in a tailored suit pass soundlessly by him in the hallway, looking like an extra from a Humphrey Bogart movie, but when he turned to ask the old man for help, the corridor was empty. The wife of one player fled with her children in the middle of the night when the taps in their bathroom repeatedly turned themselves on. John Switzer and his wife awoke one night to the sound of scratching coming from the wall behind the headboard and saw the painting above their bed come to life. It was a simple garden scene depicting a Victorian lady holding a basket with her right hand and her left resting on her chin. But now her left hand was scratching desperately at the glass as if trying to get out!

HOLIDAY INN
GRAND ISLAND, BUFFALO, NEW YORK

At the Holiday Inn, Grand Island in Buffalo, New York, many have commented on hearing what sounds like a child running along the empty halls and girlish giggling echoing in room 422. Staff have reported hearing a child calling their names and have had their duties interrupted by mischievous antics. They point out that she has been caught on camera, in the form of ghost lights which can be seen floating eerily down the corridors. Locals say that she is the ghost of a child who burned to death in a fire at the site.

GHOSTS OF NEW YORK

New York might seem to be too modern and bustling a city to offer ghosts the eerie quiet they seem to crave, but the Big Apple's skyscrapers and apartment blocks were erected on the sites of former saloons, Prohibition-era speakeasies and paupers' cemeteries known as potter's fields. So you just have to know where to look.

The Old Merchant's House at 29 East 4th Street is now a well-preserved museum with many interesting artefacts, but after dark the hapless spirit of Gertrude Tredwell, spinster daughter of a wealthy businessman, walks the empty rooms.

The 19th-century townhouses in Bay Ridge, Brooklyn, are haunted by several restless souls who pace the corridors in the early hours, their shadows passing across the frosted glass panels in the front doors of the second-floor apartments. One tenant told reporters of the night she woke to see a figure hovering over her bed and of another occasion when she felt the ice-cold touch of phantom fingers on her back.

In a Chelsea tenement, a young golden-haired girl in a lacy dress gave the living tenant's heart a jump-start when he turned over in bed to see her kneeling in prayer with her hands clasped and her head looking heavenward. As he reached to touch her hair, she vanished. The next night a man appeared in the air above a sleeping tenant and the following night the ghost of a middle-aged woman was seen staring at a blank TV screen in the same apartment, but vanished the instant the light was switched on.

SPIRITS IN A BOTTLE

There are plenty of bars where you can sit over a drink as you wait for sightings of spirits of a different kind. The intimidating spectre of Welsh poet Dylan Thomas has been seen brooding at his favourite corner table at the White Horse tavern in the West Village, where he allegedly drank himself to death in 1953.

The Bridge Café at 279 Water Street under the Brooklyn Bridge is reputedly haunted by pirates who

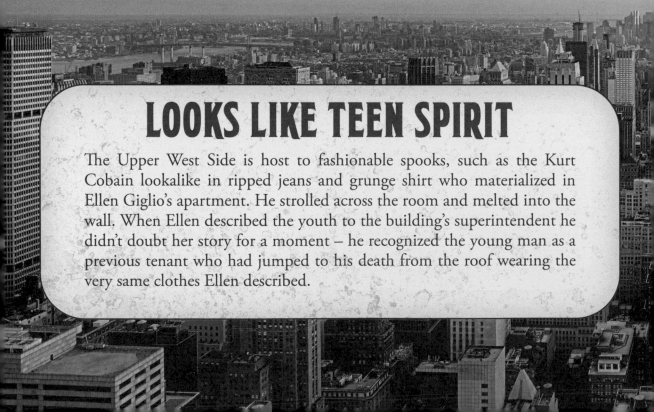

LOOKS LIKE TEEN SPIRIT

The Upper West Side is host to fashionable spooks, such as the Kurt Cobain lookalike in ripped jeans and grunge shirt who materialized in Ellen Giglio's apartment. He strolled across the room and melted into the wall. When Ellen described the youth to the building's superintendent he didn't doubt her story for a moment – he recognized the young man as a previous tenant who had jumped to his death from the roof wearing the very same clothes Ellen described.

once frequented the oldest drinking den in 'New Amsterdam'. The 19th-century Landmark Tavern on 46th Street boasts the ghosts of a Confederate soldier and an Irish serving girl, while the Manhattan Bistro on 129 Spring Street was the site of a vicious murder when a young girl, Emma Sands, was dropped down a well in what is now the basement. Her alleged murderer, Levi Weeks, was not convicted and Emma is believed to be unable to rest until he confesses to the killing.

Then there is the Chelsea Hotel, where the belligerent spirit of Sid Vicious taunts the guests; and Chumley's, a speakeasy at 86 Bedford Street, where John Steinbeck, William Faulkner and F. Scott Fitzgerald enjoyed a snifter. It is also said to be haunted by Henrietta Chumley, wife of the former owner, who drinks Manhattans with lonely barflies. Another incorporeal presence in that district of the city is Thomas Jefferson's former vice president, Aaron Burr, who still frequents the quaintly named restaurant One If By Land, Two If By Sea in Barrow Street. Aaron has been seen in the company of his daughter, Theodosia,

The ghost of former vice president Aaron Burr is said to haunt a Manhattan restaurant.

THE BIG APPLE'S BIG NAMES

The Big Apple has its share of notable historical apparitions, too. The city's last Dutch colonial governor, Peter Stuyvesant, has been sighted hopping down the dimly lit alleys of the East Village and around St Mark's in the Bowery. The Morris-Jumel Mansion at 65 Jumel Terrace was built in 1765 and is rumoured to be haunted by the ghost of its former mistress, Eliza Jumel, who glides through the rooms in a purple dress checking that windows and doors are locked. There's also the restless spirit of a young suicide victim – a servant girl who jumped from an upstairs window – and a soldier of the American Revolution whose portrait hangs on display. The spirit of author and wit Mark Twain is thought to hang out in a 19th-century brownstone building at 14 West 10th Street, where he lived briefly at the beginning of the 20th century.

The Morris-Jumel Mansion, home to the spectre of its former mistress Eliza Jumel, a serving girl and a soldier from the American Revolution.

The King's Park Psychiatric Center on Long Island houses more than a few disturbed ethereal beings.

who drowned off the coast of North Carolina en route to visit her father. The building stands on the site that was once their carriage house. Female customers at the restaurant have been robbed of their earrings by the mischievous Theodosia, and plates have been sent flying by her intemperate father, who once killed a political rival in a duel.

SHOWBIZ GHOSTS

The Dakota Building at Central Park West is haunted by the spirit of a young man and a girl in turn-of-the-century dress, while John Lennon's restless spirit has been sighted near the grimly named Undertaker's Gate.

The theatres of Times Square and Broadway are crowded with ghosts of performers and backstage staff. The Belasco Theatre is said to be haunted by the ghost of its eponymous owner, who died in 1931, but who returns to shake a clammy hand with unsuspecting thespians. The Public Theatre occasionally plays host to the spectre of Washington Irving, author of *The Legend of Sleepy Hollow*; and the Palace Theater in midtown Manhattan is believed to be inhabited by more than a hundred different ghosts. Judy Garland's ghost has been sighted standing by a private entrance and the vague impression of a little girl has been seen on the balcony, as has that of a small boy near the mezzanine. A phantom female cellist has been seen practising after hours in the orchestra pit and a haunting piano refrain has been heard in the auditorium, even though the piano lid is always locked when the instrument is not in use. Perhaps the most unsettling spirit is that of an acrobat who fell to his death during a performance. To see him is to be forewarned of one's own death.

After the evening's entertainment at New Amsterdam Theatre at 214 West 42nd Street, the ghost of Olive Thomas, a Ziegfeld Follies chorus girl, can be encountered drifting through the auditorium, a blue bottle clutched in her shadowy hand. It is thought to be the bottle of syphilis medicine prescribed for her unfaithful alcoholic husband, from which she drank a fatal dose when his womanizing had become too much for her to bear.

MORE CITY SPIRITS

Finally, most impressive of all is the derelict King's Park Psychiatric Center on Long Island, with its dozens of century-old buildings that housed the seriously disturbed and criminally insane. From its abandoned buildings, shrieks and screams can be heard by those brave enough to venture within earshot.

If you imagine that you can avoid bumping into the spirits of the old city by sticking to the modern tourist sites, think again. Some visitors to the Empire State Building in Lower Manhattan have seen more than a spectacular panorama from the viewing gallery. A young woman in 1940s clothes has been heard to say that she can't live without her fiancé, who has been killed in the war. She has been seen to throw herself off the observation platform, in spite of the high safety barriers (which were not in place till after World War II). There's no need to rush to see this performance, as she repeats it every night.

HAUNTED LONDON THEATRES

London lays claim to being the most haunted big city in the world. The cluster of theatres concentrated in the West End date back to the Elizabethan era, so it's not surprising that there are reputed to be hundreds of deceased actors, directors and backstage employees who refuse to leave the spotlight.

LYCEUM THEATRE
THE STRAND
OPENING DATE: 1765
INHABITANTS: GREY LADY

An assistant manager reported seeing a man walk out of a solid wall near the grand circle, tip his hat and bid him 'good morning' before vanishing. The ghost of a grey lady has been seen by several staff members and their descriptions of her bear an uncanny resemblance to the photograph of actress Ellen Terry, which hangs in the box office.

DOMINION THEATRE
TOTTENHAM COURT ROAD
OPENING DATE: 1929
INHABITANTS: FREDDIE MERCURY

When the Queen musical *We Will Rock You* was packing them in at the Dominion Theatre, Tottenham Court Road, the spirit of rock star Freddie Mercury was seen by several employees. Cast member Jenna Lee James claims to have felt Freddie pass through her as she was singing one of his songs, while Ian John Shillito, stage manager saw Freddie watching from the wings and criticizing aspects he didn't approve of!

PHOENIX THEATRE

CHARING CROSS ROAD
OPENING DATE: 17TH CENTURY
INHABITANTS: STEPHANIE LAWRENCE, 'EDDIE'

The aptly named Phoenix Theatre is rumoured to be haunted by the ghost of musical star Stephanie Lawrence, who died in November 2000. Deputy stage manager Richard Kingcott 'saw' her 12 years later, standing in a doorway of the set in her costume as if awaiting her entrance. On several occasions, when a character known as Eddie has been on stage, Kingcott has felt the presence of a young cast member who died tragically while essaying the role.

FORTUNE THEATRE

COVENT GARDEN
OPENING DATE: 1924
INHABITANTS: STAGE SPECTRE

The Fortune Theatre was haunted by a ghost during a long-running production of the supernatural thriller *The Woman in Black*. The most unnerving aspect was that the real apparition and the stage spectre looked uncannily alike. Natalie Block, the actress who had taken the role of the ghost, saw a woman sitting motionless watching the play, wearing a turn-of-the-century corseted dress. The young male lead experienced considerable anxiety as he watched her walk off stage into the outstretched arms of the ghost!

PALACE THEATRE

SHAFTESBURY AVENUE
OPENING DATE: 1891
INHABITANTS: ANNA PAVLOVA

The Palace Theatre is home to a curious apparition – the torso of a ballerina which emerges from the floor of the stage to perform an arabesque. It is believed to be the world-famous ballet dancer Anna Pavlova, who appeared there regularly.

THEATRE ROYAL

HAYMARKET
OPENING DATE: 1905
INHABITANTS: JOHN BALDWIN BUCKSTONE

The 300-year-old Theatre Royal is reputed to be haunted by comic actor-manager John Baldwin Buckstone, whose disembodied voice and footsteps have been heard in what was once his dressing room. In 1949, Sir Donald Sinden and actress Gillian Howell saw a man in a long, grey Victorian morning coat standing near Sir Ralph Richardson's dressing room. A few minutes later, as they waited in the wings, they saw Richardson on stage,

so Sinden rushed back up the stairs to check, but the mysterious figure had vanished. Dame Judi Dench saw a man in a long tailcoat hurrying ahead of her, but when she turned the corner, he was nowhere to be seen. The theatre's master carpenter saw a phantom dressed in a cloak and top hat one night who abruptly vanished.

THEATRE ROYAL

DRURY LANE

OPENING DATE: 17TH CENTURY

INHABITANTS: 'MAN IN GREY', JOSEPH GRIMALDI

The oldest theatre in the West End, the Theatre Royal, hosts more ghosts than its neighbours. Its most famous inhabitant is an 18th-century aristocrat known as the 'Man in Grey'. This gentleman always appears in a powdered wig and a tricorne hat, immaculately attired in a jacket, cloak and riding boots and carrying a sword. He is believed to be the ghost of a murder victim whose remains were discovered in the building. The Theatre Royal is also home to the mischievous spirit of Joseph Grimaldi, the 'father' of modern clowns.

ALDWYCH THEATRE

DRURY LANE

OPENING DATE: 1905

INHABITANTS: 'WILLY WONKA'

Staff at the Aldwych Theatre have complained of poltergeist activity such as doors opening unaided, the sound of a woman weeping and spirit lights

or orbs floating through the auditorium. When psychic Becky Walsh investigated the Aldwych, she 'saw' the image of a gentleman dressed in a Willy Wonka costume with a top hat and cane – matching a photograph produced by hotel staff of Seymour Hicks.

THE TOWN TOO TOUGH TO DIE

They called Tombstone, Arizona, 'The Town Too Tough To Die' and it appears that some of its most notorious inhabitants are equally reluctant to go quietly. The town is now preserved as a national museum with many of the old buildings lovingly restored to their former rickety glory and stocked with original artefacts from its violent past including the hearse that transported bodies to Boot Hill, the hangman's noose and the honky-tonk piano which accompanied many a bar-room brawl. Some say that if you stay after closing time you can hear the piano playing 'Red River Valley', the cowboys' favourite tune, and hear the echo of their raucous laughter.

The streets of Tombstone were the setting for numerous showdowns. Some of the meanest gunfighters of the old West did their hardest drinking and gambling in the town's notorious Bird Cage Theatre, which also served as a saloon. As many as 31 ghosts are thought to haunt the saloon which was the site of 26 killings – a fact borne out by the 140 bullet holes that can be seen peppering the ceiling. The spook most frequently seen in the saloon is a stagehand dressed in black striped trousers, wearing a card dealer's visor and carrying a clipboard. He is said to appear from nowhere, walk across the stage and exit through the facing wall. Tourists have also reported seeing the ghost of a young boy who had died of yellow fever in 1882 and heard an unidentified woman sighing plaintively as if pining for her lost love. Others have commented on the authenticity of the actors' clothes in the gambling parlour and the dancehall, only to be told that the museum doesn't employ actors, nor does it ask its staff to dress in period costumes.

A strong smell of cigar smoke lingers round the card tables and there is the delicate scent of lilac perfume in the backstage bathroom. Equally odd is the $100 poker chip which mysteriously appeared on the poker table one day then promptly vanished after being locked away in a desk before turning up in a filing cabinet some days later. The ghosts seem to enjoy playing hide and seek with small but significant items. Furniture has moved by itself and one member of the museum staff was physically attacked by a mischievous spirit who hit the tour guide on the back of the knee, causing him to fall to the floor.

Unattended still cameras have fired off exposures by themselves and have altered focus in the middle of shooting before resetting themselves correctly. However, it seems the ghosts can register on electrical equipment if their emission is strong enough. Small balls of light have been captured on film floating up from the floor and a face has been seen in the large painting which hangs behind the bar. One female member of staff who works in the gift shop on the ground floor of the Bird Cage Theatre swears she once saw on a security monitor a lady in a white dress walking through the cellar at closing time.

The notorious Bird Cage Theatre of Tombstone, Arizona, in 1946.

Tombstone, 1885. The town suffered two major fires in 1881 and 1882. Those, with the decline in the silver mines, meant that by the mid-1880s the place was virtually abandoned.

TOMBSTONE'S SPOOKY SITES

Other haunted sites in Tombstone include Nellie Cashman's Restaurant, where customers and employees have reported seeing dishes crash to the floor, and Schiefflin Hall where rowdy town council meetings were held in the 1880s. At the Wells Fargo stage stop ghostly drivers and phantom passengers have been seen alighting from a spectral stagecoach on their way to the Grand Hotel. Residents and tourists have also reported seeing a man in a black frock coat who starts walking across the street but never appears on the other side and traffic often stops for a woman in white who committed suicide after her child died of fever in the 1880s. Visitors' photographs taken on Boot Hill of their relatives standing in front of the gravestones appeared to show the faint but unmistakable image of a cowboy in period costume in the background.

THE GHOSTS OF GLASTONBURY

Glastonbury is one of the most sacred and mysterious sites in Britain, and of great spiritual significance to mystically minded Christians and pagans alike. Legend has it that King Arthur and Queen Guinevere are buried within the ruins of Glastonbury Abbey and that the Holy Grail, the chalice from which Jesus is said to have drunk on the night before his crucifixion, is hidden nearby. But of all the legends associated with Glastonbury the most extraordinary and controversial is that concerning the discovery of the ruins of the abbey itself.

In 1907, architect and archaeologist Frederick Bligh Bond (1864–1945) was appointed director of excavations by the Church of England and charged with the task of unearthing the abbey ruins which several previous incumbents had spent their lives searching for in vain. The work was unpaid, but Bligh had a thriving architectural practice in Bristol and he viewed the search for the abbey as an almost mystical mission. He was confident that he would succeed where the others had failed for he believed that he had an uncommon advantage over his predecessors.

His interest in paranormal phenomena had led him to join the Society for Psychical Research through which he had met Captain John Allen Bartlett, an eager advocate of automatic writing. Together the two men took up pen and paper in the hope of pinpointing the location of the ruins by tapping into what Carl Jung had called the Collective Unconscious.

The quality of the messages they received swiftly persuaded them that they were in communication with separate discarnate personalities, quite possibly the ghosts of long dead monks who had lived in the monastery.

At the first session, which took place in November 1907, the two men sat opposite each other across an empty table in reverent expectation. Bartlett took the part of the medium and Bond the 'sitter'. This involved Bond asking the questions while placing two fingers on the back of Bartlett's hand to make a connection with the spirits.

'Can you tell us anything about Glastonbury?' asked the architect, to which an invisible force answered in a legible scrawl by animating Bartlett's hand: 'All knowledge is eternal and is available to mental sympathy.'

The connection had been made and information as to the location of the chapels and other buried structures was freely given in a mixture of Latin and

English by a disembodied spirit who identified himself as a 15th-century monk named Brother William (possibly William of Malmesbury).

To Bond and Bartlett's delight the 'monk' and his companions, known as 'The Watchers', supplied very detailed information regarding the location of the abbey's foundations. When the excavations started, often the workmen would simply have to dig a few feet down to

The ruins of Glastonbury Abbey.

hit the precise spot, after which the archaeologists would move in and begin sifting the soil for artefacts. Needless to say, Bond's benefactors were beside themselves and the full extent of the ancient site was revealed over dozens of sessions during the next five years.

By 1917, Bond felt justly proud in having uncovered one of Britain's most sacred sites and decided to tell his story in print. But when *The Gates of Remembrance* was published in 1918, the Church condemned it and strenuously denied that anything other than conventional methods had been used to unearth the abbey. In an effort to distance themselves from Bond they terminated his employment, banned him from ever setting foot within the grounds again and ordered that his guidebook to Glastonbury be removed from the shelves of the gift shop.

GHOSTS OF THE LONDON UNDERGROUND

When the original underground tunnels were excavated during the Victorian era several historic graveyards were destroyed to make way for the network, and it is believed that their inhabitants were none too pleased at having their eternal rest disturbed. Other historic sites including gaols, paupers' graves and, most significantly, 17th-century plague pits were wilfully destroyed in the name of progress.

During the construction of St Pancras station the Church complained that the reburying of caskets at the site of an old cemetery was being carried out in haste and with disrespect for the dead. As recently as the 1960s the construction of the new Victoria line had to be delayed when a boring machine tore through a plague pit, unearthing the corpses and traumatizing several brawny navvies.

If you add to this the number of poor souls who have committed suicide by throwing themselves under trains and those who have perished in disasters, you have a real-life ghost train experience waiting for the unwary traveller.

Sarah Whitehead, the 'Black Nun'.

01 BANK

When Bank station was built, workmen are said to have disturbed the restless spirit of Sarah Whitehead, known locally as the 'Black Nun'. In life she was the sister of a bank cashier who had been executed for forgery in 1811. She acquired her nickname from the commuters who saw her dressed in black waiting, every evening for 40 years until her death, outside the bank where he had worked.

Merchant seaman and tea planter turned actor, William Terriss or 'Breezy Bill' as he was known, was stabbed to death by a deranged and out-of-work actor in December, 1897.

02 COVENT GARDEN

Staff at Covent Garden demanded a transfer to another station in the 1950s after a tall Edwardian gentleman in a frock coat, top hat and wearing opera gloves appeared unannounced in their restroom. It is thought that he might be the actor William Terriss, who was stabbed to death outside the Adelphi Theatre in the Strand in 1897. The station was built on the site of a bakery which the actor patronized en route to rehearsals.

03 ALDWYCH

This station was built on the site of the Royal Strand Theatre and was said to be haunted by the ghost of an actress who hungers for applause. Closed in 1994, Aldwych had a higher than average turnover of cleaning and maintenance staff as dozens refused to work there after being confronted by a 'figure' which suddenly appeared on the tracks inside one of the approach tunnels without warning.

04 FARRINGDON

Of all the London Underground stations, Farringdon is the one to avoid if you are travelling alone. It is the haunt of the 'Screaming Spectre', a vengeful young apprentice hat maker who was murdered in 1758 by her master and his daughter.

06 HIGHGATE

Highgate underground station is in the vicinity of the famous cemetery of the same name, a place that guarantees some serious spectral activity. Contrary to popular belief, ghosts do not linger around their graves as they do not want to be reminded that they are dead or how they met their end. Instead they 'commute' to where they can relive their routine lives and for many recently deceased Londoners this means their home, office and the Tube network. And you thought the trains were overcrowded with the living! Curiously, local residents claim to be able to hear the sound of trains running through an abandoned and overgrown cutting that was intended to connect with the Northern line when the station was extended in 1941.

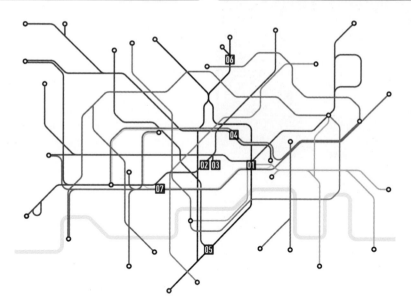

05 ELEPHANT & CASTLE

After closing time, when the station falls silent, the night staff have reported hearing phantom steps, inexplicable rapping sounds and doors banging shut. It is believed the platforms are haunted by the ghost of a traveller who was in such haste that he tripped and fell under an oncoming train.

07 SOUTH KENSINGTON

The only reported sighting of a ghost train was made by a passenger in December 1928. The commuter claimed to have heard the screech of its brakes and to have seen a phantom figure dressed in an Edwardian smoking jacket and peaked cap clinging to the side of the engine just moments before it was swallowed up in the darkness of the tunnel.

HAUNTED HOLLYWOOD

Living legends die hard, particularly those whose larger-than-life personalities dominated the silver screen in Hollywood's heyday. Hollywood Memorial Cemetery (recently renamed Hollywood Forever) is the oldest graveyard in Tinseltown and is reputed to be uncommonly active as far as spectral sightings are concerned.

Paramount Studios is said to be haunted by the ghosts of its most enduring stars, Douglas Fairbanks and Rudolph Valentino. The most remarkable incident occurred one evening when a technician fell 20 ft (6 m) from a lighting gantry and was apparently saved from certain death by a spectral Samaritan who broke his fall. He seemed to hover in the air just inches from the ground for an instant, before dropping to the floor, unharmed, in full view of his startled colleagues.

After his death at the age of 31, Rudolph Valentino became the most active ghost in Hollywood. His spirit glides elegantly through the rooms of his former mansion, the Falcon's Lair. Staff at Paramount studios have sworn they have seen 'the Sheik' admiring the stock in the costume department and walking soundlessly through Studio Five. The ghost of a lady admirer in a veil is often seen bringing phantom flowers to the star's tomb at the Hollywood Forever cemetery.

At Culver City Studios, carpenters speak in whispers of a grey figure dressed in a jacket and tie and sporting a fedora hat who walks right through them and disappears through a door in the facing wall. From the description he appears to be the restless spirit of former studio boss Thomas Ince, who died in suspicious circumstances in 1924.

Another haunted studio is Universal, which was the setting for the original silent version of *Phantom of the Opera* (1925) starring horror screen legend Lon Chaney Sr, whose spirit has been seen scampering along the catwalks and gantries with his cape billowing behind.

TV's original Superman, actor George Reeves, is said to have shot himself at his Beverly Hills home in 1959, three days before his wedding, because he could not cope with being typecast. His friends and family maintain that he was murdered. Visitors to the house have reported sensing his apparition dressed in his Superman costume. Another mysterious murder/suicide was that of Thelma Todd who died in 1935 in the garage of her beachside café on the Pacific Coast Highway, near Malibu. The police suspected a suicide, but there were bloodstains which were never satisfactorily explained. The present owners of the property claim to have seen her ghost on the premises and to have smelt exhaust fumes in the empty garage.

The Vogue Theatre, Hollywood Boulevard, is said to be haunted by a projectionist who collapsed and died in the projection booth, a maintenance engineer, and a schoolteacher and her pupils who were burned to death at their school, Prospect Elementary.

Other haunted Hollywood locations include the Roosevelt Hotel, where guests have complained of hearing a clarinet playing in the early hours only to be told that it is the resident ghost of screen star Montgomery Clift. More unsettling is the case of the haunted mirror which used to take pride of place in

The ghost of horror legend Lon Chaney Sr haunts Universal Studios to this day.

Newspapers proclaiming the death of Marilyn Monroe, 6 August 1962.

a room Marilyn Monroe had stayed in. Long after Marilyn's death a cleaner suffered the shock of seeing Monroe's face appear in the mirror.

Some ghosts had too good a time during their life to waste the afterlife wailing and moaning. Writer, director and bon vivant Orson Welles continues to enjoy brandy and cigars at his favourite table in Sweet Lady Jane's Restaurant in Hollywood. Fellow diners comment on the smell of cigar smoke but the maître d'hôtel refuses to give a refund.

Actor Hugh Grant is said to have heard the ghost of Bette Davis sobbing and moaning as it sweeps through the luxury apartments in Los Angeles' Colonial Building, while comedian Lucille Ball is said to haunt her home at 100 North Roxbury Drive; windows have been broken in the Ball house, furniture has moved of its own accord and shouting has been traced to an empty attic. *Ghostbusters* star Dan Aykroyd was unnerved when he realized he was sharing his bed with the ghost of the singer Mama Cass Elliot.

Bette Davis is said to haunt the rooms of Los Angeles' Colonial Building, where she lived for many years.

AFTERWORD

There is a saying I have heard often when talking to the various psychics and paranormal researchers I have worked with and interviewed over the past 30 years or more. 'For those who believe, no proof is necessary; for those who don't, no proof is enough.'

It is my understanding that the spirit world and the physical world co-exist and that we can all glimpse this other dimension, this other reality because we are all psychic to various degrees. Clairvoyants and mediums are different from the average person only in that they are aware that they possess this innate ability, or sensitivity, and have chosen to develop it by being uncommonly receptive to these subtle impressions from the 'other side' and trusting in their intuition.

Others may glimpse the inhabitants of this other reality under certain conditions without having made a conscious effort to do so. In this book I have given numerous examples of both and hope that it has provided those who believe in ghosts with much to support and justify their convictions and for those who did not believe, with sufficient grounds to question their doubts and reserve judgement until they see a ghost for themselves!

Those who deny the possibility of the supernatural do so partly out of fear and partly on principle, believing that the logical and scientific mind should discount what they consider to be nothing more than an irrational superstition. They argue, and with some justification, that the presence of ghosts has never been proven and that other paranormal phenomena have not been replicated under laboratory conditions. However, heightened states of consciousness and the incorporeal cannot be measured, recorded or filmed. Brain waves and heart rates can be measured, but thoughts and emotions cannot. It is the same with ghosts which appear to be either our disembodied consciousness or residual emotions in the ether.

However, most us cannot live in a world of spirits and the supernatural because we need to be grounded in the 'real' world to fulfil our responsibilities and in doing so we find stability and a certain security. That is both understandable and desirable, but if we live entirely in the material world which is by nature transient and superficial, then we are sleepwalking through life and oblivious to the multi-dimensional world in which we exist.

Believing in ghosts and other manifestations of the supernatural and paranormal is not, therefore, an escape from reality as the sceptics would have us believe, but quite the opposite. It is to truly see what wonders and potential dangers we live amongst.

Having explored many aspects of the paranormal and written several books on the subject, I thought I had the paranormal pretty well sussed, as they say. I had my beliefs, based largely on personal experience and those of psychics and mediums I had worked with, but also my doubts about other aspects, specifically spirit photography. Until that is, a member of my family happened to mention having seen a photograph that her teenage daughter had taken at a children's birthday party in 2005. It had been passed around the group of friends, all of whom remarked on the presence of a little girl in Victorian dress who could be seen peeping out from under the legs of one of the children. This was not the typical faint blurry image one associates with alleged 'ghost photos', but a sharp unmistakable image of a little girl with blond ringlets who nobody could identify. It had been a small party in a private house so there was no chance for an uninvited guest to sneak in unnoticed. Everyone in the photo knew one another, with the exception of the unidentified child. What is even more remarkable is that when the photograph had been taken, one of the children had run screaming from the room and had to be comforted by her mother. It wasn't until the photograph was developed that the hosts understood the reason for her fear. The distressed girl must have seen the ghost.

So, I no longer dismiss the possibility of such phenomena out of hand, although I maintain a healthy scepticism with regard to some of the more dramatic claims.

Examining the paranormal is not an escape from reality – it is an engagement with the many dimensions that affect our lives that stretch beyond the material realm.

INDEX

PICTURE CREDITS

t = top, b = bottom, l = left, r = right, m = middle

AKG Images: 88

Alamy: 31, 37, 53, 155t, 176bl, 179t

Brooklyn Museum: 140

Corbis: 15bl, 28, 42, 73, 74r, 80, 86, 97, 101, 103, 127, 162, 168, 174t, 180tl, 186, 196, 200b, 203b, 204

Copyright of Darren Kyle O'Neill: 109 (Bill Stoneham)

Getty Images: 61, 113, 203t

Mary Evans: 38, 39t, 40, 41, 43, 57, 59, 74l, 81, 82, 137, 146r, 157

Metropolitan Museum of Art, New York: 52

NASA: 65

National Portrait Gallery, USA: 46

Science Photo Library: 89

Shutterstock: 6, 8, 10, 11, 12, 13l, 14, 18, 19, 20, 25, 34, 39b, 56, 62, 63, 66, 67r, 75, 76, 78, 85, 90, 91, 95, 99, 100t, 104, 106, 110, 111, 112, 114, 116, 120 (x2), 122, 124, 128, 129, 130 (x2), 131, 134, 144, 151, 152, 154 (x2), 158, 160, 161, 164, 167, 172, 175 (x2), 176tl, 176tr, 176br, 177tl, 177tr, 177br, 179b, 180tr, 180b, 183, 185, 188, 190, 192 (x3), 193l, 194t, 195 (x3), 199, 201

Topfoto: 118, 119, 155b, 156, 171, 174b, 197

Unsplash: 4, 22

Wikimedia Commons: 13r, 15br, 16, 17, 27, 30, 32, 33, 44, 45, 47, 48, 49, 50, 51, 54 (x2), 55, 58, 66l, 68, 69, 71, 83, 93, 96, 139, 143, 146l, 147, 148, 149, 163, 176tm, 177m, 177bl, 178, 184, 189, 191, 193r, 194b, 200t, 202

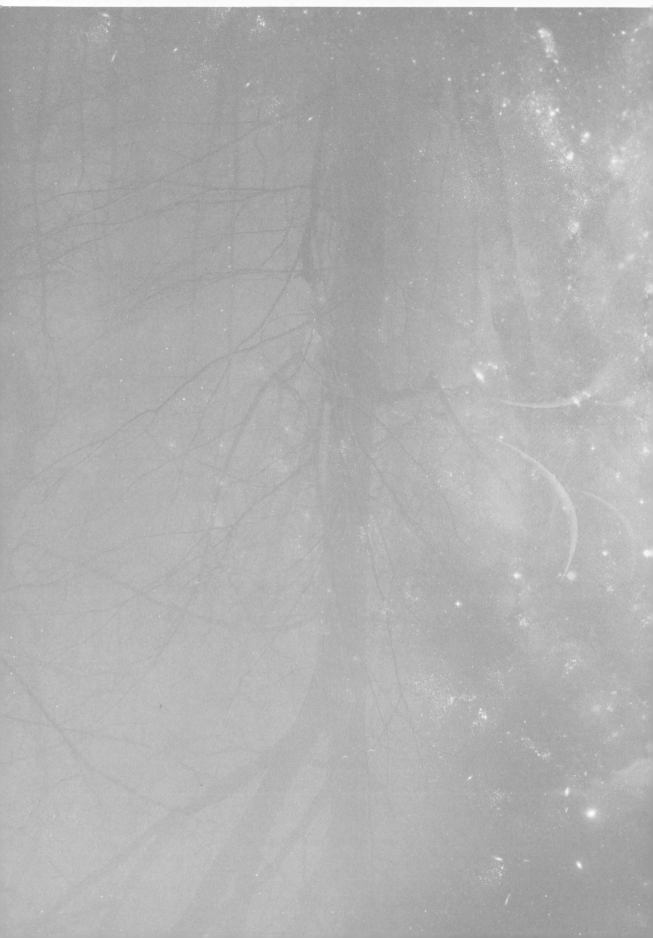